Includes authentic video from the BBC

British 3
News
Update

Timothy Knowles   Mayumi Tamura
Minne Tanaka   Mihoko Nakamura

KINSEIDO

Kinseido Publishing Co., Ltd.
3-21 Kanda Jimbo-cho, Chiyoda-ku,
Tokyo 101-0051, Japan

First published 2021 by Kinseido Publishing Co., Ltd.

Text design & Editorial support C-leps Co., Ltd.

News clips ©BBC 2020.
Images ©BBC 2020.
Cover images ©BBC 2020.

This edition produced under license by Kinseido Publishing Co., Ltd.2021.

BBCニュース ホームページ：www.bbc.com/news

Introduction

The British Broadcasting Corporation (BBC) is internationally famous for the quality and impartiality of its news items. BBC reporters also strive to make the news both interesting and as easy to understand as possible. In this book we have chosen 15 items that we think would be of particular interest. Most are about Britain, as you might expect, but many of the issues covered, such as health, education, and the environment are generally familiar to Japanese learners. There are also some important international issues, and topics that are included because they give a fascinating insight into a different culture.

It is hoped that the items will be motivating, and that students will be eager to watch and listen because they are interested in what they are discovering. New and important items of vocabulary are introduced, and the notes (in Japanese) will explain any interesting and important points of grammar and usage of English. However, perhaps the most important purpose of this book is that the learners should be able to engage in the subject matter, and then discuss it and research it together. With this in mind, we have developed discussion questions that would encourage them to relate these new discoveries with what is already familiar to them in Japan.

Finally, it is important to keep up with the technology that is now available to students. Therefore, videos are now easily accessible online. This will make it easy for students to study by themselves out of class.

We hope you enjoy the book and the videos.

はじめに

　本書は、実際に放送されたBBC（英国放送協会）のニュースを教材として、ニュースキャスターや街頭インタヴューを受ける native speaker が自然に話す英語に触れることで、学習者のリスニング力や語彙力といった英語力を伸ばすことを目的としています。同時に、イギリスや世界で起こっている出来事やその背景となる社会や文化についても学べるように工夫されています。

　扱うトピックは、政治、経済、環境など多岐にわたるものとし、できるだけ up to date でありつつも、普遍的なものを選びました。学習する皆様の興味関心の幅を広げ、ご希望にお応えすることができれば幸いです。

　前作に引き続き、ユニット内のコラムは、イギリス文化についての面白い情報を増やして充実を図り、Questions も最初の **Setting the Scene** に始まり、**Follow Up** にいたるまで、各ユニットで取り上げるニュースを順序良く掘り下げて理解が深まるように配慮しました。

　本書を通じて、伝統と革新が共存する多民族国家イギリスが、4 つの地域の独自性を保ちつつ、総体としてのイギリスらしさ（"Britishness"）を模索する今の姿を見ていただけると思います。現在のイギリスは、EU からの離脱やスコットランドの独立などの多くの問題を抱えており、日本や世界に与える影響を考慮すると、今後もその動きから目が離せません。

　このテキストを使って学習する皆様が、イギリスや世界の状勢に興味を持ち、さらには、自分から英語ニュースに触れたり、英語で意見を述べたりと、ますます学習の場が広がっていきますことを、執筆者一同願っております。

　最後になりましたが、本書の作成にあたり、BBC ニュースを教材として使うことを許可してくださいましたBBC、編集に際してご尽力いただきました金星堂の長島吉成様とシー・レップスの佐伯亜希様に、この場をお借りして心より感謝申し上げます。

テキストの特徴

　普段の生活の中で、ニュースの英語に触れる機会はあまりないかもしれません。本テキストは、初めて英語でニュースを観る場合でも無理なく取り組めるよう、多種多様なアクティビティを用意しています。単語のチェックや内容確認、穴埋め、要約、ディスカッションを通して、段階を踏みながらニュースを理解できるような作りになっているので、達成感を感じることができるでしょう。

Starting Off

1. Setting the Scene

　実際にニュースを観る前に、ニュースで扱われるトピックについて考えるためのセクションです。トピックについての学習を始めるにあたり、身近な問題としてトピックを捉えられるような問題を用意しました。ここで先にニュースに関する情報を整理しておけば、実際にニュースを観る際に理解が容易になります。ニュースで使われている単語や語句、または重要な概念をここで予習しておきましょう。

2. Building Language

　ニュースの中で使われる重要単語を学びます。単に日本語の訳語を覚えるのではなく、英語での定義を通して、また同義語を覚えながら、単語の持つ意味を英語で理解することを目指します。また、これらの単語はディスカッションを行うときにもおそらく頻繁に使うことになる単語ですし、ニュースの核となる単語ですので、発音もしっかりと確認することが重要です。

Watching the News

3. Understanding Check 1

　実際にニュースの中身を詳しく見ていく前に、どんな意見が交わされているのかを確認します。ここで具体的にニュースのイメージをつかむことが大事です。全体像を簡単にでも把握することで、ニュース理解の大きな助けとなります。

4. Understanding Check 2

　ニュースに関する問題を解くことで、どれだけニュースを理解できたか確認することができます。間違えた箇所に関しては、なぜ間違えたのかをしっかりと分析し、内容を正確に把握しましょう。**Filling Gaps** のアクティビティを行ってから **Understanding Check 2** に取り組むのも効果的かもしれません。

5. Filling Gaps

　ニュースの中で重要な意味を持つ単語を聞き取ります。何度も繰り返し聞き、正しい発音を意識します。それと同時に、単語を正しく書き取ることで、耳と手との両方の動きを通して重要単語を習得することを目指します。もし時間に余裕があれば、穴埋めの単語を実際に発音し、耳と手に加え口も使って覚えると効果的です。

Moving On

6. Making a Summary

　この箇所は、これまで観てきたニュースをまとめる部分でもあり、かつ **Follow Up** に至る前の準備の段階でもあります。しっかりと内容を理解しているか、このアクティビティを通して確認しましょう。また、**Building Language** で出てきた単語を再度使っているため、単語の習熟の確認ができるようになっています。

7. Follow Up

　ニュースと関連したトピックをいくつか挙げてあります。ニュースで得た知識、また単語を活かして話し合いを行うためのセクションです。トピックには、その場で話し合えるものと各自調べてから発表し合うもの、両方が含まれています。そのニュースに関してだけでなく、今後似たような話題に接したときにも意見を述べることができるよう、このアクティビティで仕上げを行います。

Background Information

　ニュースでは、必ずしもすべての事柄が説明されているとは限りません。ニュースの核となる事柄で、かつニュースの中ではあまり詳しく説明されていないことに関して、このセクションでは補足しています。ニュースをより深く理解するのにも役立ちますし、**Follow Up** での話し合いの際にも使えるかもしれません。

Behind the Scenes

　ニュースに関連することではありますが、**Background Information** とは異なりここではニュースの核となることではなく、話題が広がる知識、教養が深まる知識を取り上げました。肩の力を抜き、楽しんで読めるような内容になっています。

- ・　各ユニットで取り上げたニュース映像はオンラインで視聴することができます。詳しくは巻末を参照ください。
- ・　テキスト準拠の Audio CD には、各ユニットのニュース音声と、ニュースを学習用に聞き取りやすく吹き替えた音声、Making a Summary を収録しています。

Contents

Map of The United Kingdom

正式名称は **The United Kingdom of Great Britain and Northern Ireland**（グレートブリテン及び北アイルランド連合王国）。**England**（イングランド）、**Wales**（ウェールズ）、**Scotland**（スコットランド）、**Northern Ireland**（北アイルランド）の4国から成る連合国家です（2020年現在）。

※（　）は本テキストでその地名、場所が登場するユニットを表します

Unit 1

Less Plastic at Glastonbury

熱気高まる野外フェスの会場に観客が列をなしていますが、皆、何かを手にしています。熱い日差しを乗り切るためのエコな工夫について、ニュースを見てみましょう。

Starting Off

1 Setting the Scene

▶ **What do you think?**

1. Have you ever been to a music festival? Tell your partner about it.
2. Why do you think so many people go to music festivals?
3. When thousands of people attend a festival, what problems do you think there might be?

2 Building Language

▶ **Which word (1-6) best fits which explanation (a-f)?**

1. urge   [   ]   a. a person who is selling something
2. soar   [   ]   b. the process of absorbing or drinking enough water
3. hydration   [   ]   c. rise or increase very rapidly
4. dotted   [   ]   d. scattered or placed, apparently at random
5. vendor   [   ]   e. the idea that pleasure is most important
6. hedonism   [   ]   f. recommend or encourage somebody to do something

Watching the News

3 Understanding Check 1

▶ **Read the quotes, then watch the news and match them to the right people.**

1. ... I think the festival needs to look at that and do what they can to prevent that ...   [   ]

2. Usually I'd be drinking out of plastic bottles ...   [   ]

3. It's all about refill and reuse. [   ]

4. Normally pop to an ice-cream van ...
                                        [   ]

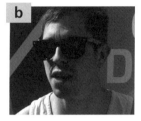

4 Understanding Check 2

▶ **Which is the best answer?**

1. These are all problems related to the Glastonbury Festival. Which one was <u>not</u> mentioned?
    a. Festival-goers leave their tents behind.
    b. There are long queues for the toilets.
    c. Festival-goers need a lot of water.
    d. People can get burnt by the sun.

2. What <u>can't</u> festival-goers do at the festival this year?
    a. buy ice-cream
    b. use metal cups
    c. buy plastic bottles
    d. fill their bottles with water

3. How many water taps are there on the site this year?
    a. over 870
    b. about 500
    c. about 20
    d. hundreds of thousands

▶ **What do you remember?**

4. Why are there long queues at the water stations?

_____

5. What is the difference between the women's behaviour last year and their behaviour this year?

_____

6. What does the founder of Extinction Rebellion think that the festival needs to do?

_____

╭──────────────── **BACKGROUND INFORMATION** ────────────────╮

　今回のニュースは、2019年のグラストンベリー・フェスティバル (Glastonbury Festival) で、使い捨てペットボトルの使用が禁止されたという話題でした。グラストンベリー・フェスティバルは、1970年から南西イングランドのピルトンで行われている大規模野外フェスティバルです。第1回の来場者は1,500人、入場料は農場の無料の牛乳が付いて1ポンドでしたが、その人気と規模は拡大の一途をたどり、2019年は6月26日から30日の5日間の開催で、20万3,000人の来場者を迎え、入場料は248ポンド(約34,720円、1ポンド＝140円)になりました。

　2019年のグラストンベリー・フェスティバルは、「気候変動と環境 (Climate Change and the Environment)」をテーマに掲げ、ニュースにあったように、使い捨てペットボトルの使用を禁止しました。また、著名な動物学者、植物学者、プロデューサーのサー・デイヴィッド・アッテンボロー (Sir David Attenborough, 1926-) が、メインとなるピラミッド・ステージ (the Pyramid Stage) で気候変動活動への関与を強める発言をし、地球温暖化や生物の絶滅に反対する市民活動団体であるエクスティンクション・レベリオンが、気候変動の回避を訴えるエクスティンクション・パレード (Extinction Procession) を行ったりしました。他にも、毎年1,300人のリサイクル・ボランティアが参加したり、フェスティバルに参加する人の約40%が、グラストンベリーに自家用車ではなく公共交通機関を使ってやって来たりと、環境問題への配慮が見られます。

　今回のフェスティバル終了後、主催者側は、ごみ箱や地面にペットボトルが一切捨てられておらず、プラスチックごみが大幅に削減されたと発表しましたが、その一方で、数千のペットボトルが地面に捨てられている現場写真も残されており、なおも改善が求められています。さらに、50周年を記念するはずだった2020年のフェスは新型コロナウイルスの感染拡大の影響で中止となり、今後は大勢の人々が集まるフェスにおける感染対策も課題になっています。

参考：

https://www.glastonburyfestivals.co.uk/
https://rebellion.earth/
https://www.bbc.com/news/uk-england-somerset-48823850

╰───╯

Unit 1 Less Plastic at Glastonbury　　3

5 Filling Gaps | News Story | CD1-02 [Original] CD1-03 [Voiced]

▶ Watch the news, then fill the gaps in the text.

Newsreader: Festival-goers at Glastonbury are being (**1**) to protect themselves from the sun, with record temperatures forecast over the weekend. And they're also being (**2**) to drink plenty of water, but, for the first time, organisers have (**3**) the sale of plastic bottles at the festival. Fiona Lamdin reports now from Glastonbury.

5

Fiona Lamdin: As temperatures (**4**) into the twenties, Worthy Farm and its festival-goers are in need of (**5**), and not surprisingly, queues have been building at all the water stations (**6**) around the festival.

10

Lamdin: For the first time Glastonbury have banned the sale of (**7**) plastic. There's over 870 taps on site. It's all about refill and reuse.

Man: Usually I'd be drinking out of plastic bottles, um, because most of the (**8**) would be selling them on site. But they're not selling them this year, so (**9**) I bought a £5 metal cup, and you can refill it at any of the water points. There's loads of them on site, so it's easy.

15

First woman: It's nice that you don't have the option to buy plastic bottles as well, so everybody's (**10**) it completely.

20

Second woman: Yeah.

Third woman: Normally pop to an ice-cream van and buy a few bottles of water, as well as lemonade and that kind of thing. So this year we've (**11**) to bring our own bottles.

Lamdin: Last year more than a million plastic bottles were (**12**) at the festival. And this is where they all came.

25

Lamdin: And already it's made a (**13**) difference. There's (**14**) less plastic than there was last festival.

Lamdin: With hundreds of thousands traveling here, and the mountain of tents often (**15**) (**16**), the founder of the climate change campaign group, Extinction Rebellion, worries about its impact.

30

Dr. Gail Bradbrook, co-founder of Extinction Rebellion: I'm sure it's got a (¹⁷   ) footprint. And, it is a piece of (¹⁸   ), isn't it? It's people having a good time. Er, but from that can come quite a narcissistic side to ourselves, where we're not really looking

at what we're doing. And so when, in-, individuals walk away and leave a load of (¹⁹   ) behind, single-use tents, I mean how (²⁰   ) is that? Er, so I think the festival needs to look at that and do what they can to prevent that, and also the individuals that are here.

Lamdin: A future (²¹   ) for this festival. But for now, at least, even the police are (²²   ) (²³   ) the new Glastonbury rules. Organisers hope, as people leave, they'll not only take their (²⁴   ), but the festival's message. Fiona Lamdin, BBC news.

(Friday 28 June 2019)

Notes

l.1 **Glastonbury**「グラストンベリー」グラストンベリー・フェスティバル（Glastonbury Festival）を指す。イングランドのサマセット州で行われる大規模な野外フェス。1970年より開催　l.10 **Worthy Farm**「ワージー・ファーム」グラストンベリー・フェスティバルの会場となる農場　l.33 **Extinction Rebellion**「エクスティンクション・レベリオン」気候変動の緩和や環境保護のための活動を行っている団体。環境活動家のロジャー・ハラム（Roger Hallam）、ゲイル・ブラッドブルックらによって2018年にイギリスで設立された

ᗷᴇʜɪɴᴅ ᴛʜᴇ Sᴄᴇɴᴇs

納屋の音楽会

　グラストンベリー・フェスティバルは、ヒッピー文化たけなわの1970年に、ワージー・ファームの農園主夫妻によって始められ、妻亡き後は娘が手伝って、家族経営で続けられてきました。農園がコンサート会場になっていますが、畜産業の盛んなイギリスでは、家畜を収容する広い納屋は田舎の風物詩で、その空間を利用した音楽会もよく行われます。厩で生まれたイエス・キリストの生誕劇や、クリスマス・キャロルのコンサートは、クリスマス・シーズンに人気の催しです。

Moving On

6 Making a Summary

 CD1-04

▶ **Fill the gaps to complete the summary.**

　Hundreds of thousands of people go to Glastonbury Festival every year, and last year they bought more than a million plastic bottles from (v　　　　　　) on the site. These were just left behind and recycled. This year, even though temperatures have (s　　　　　　), and festival-goers must drink lots of water to stay (h　　　　　　), organisers have banned the sale of plastic bottles. Instead, they have (u　　　　　　) people to fill their own bottles or cups from one of the 870 water taps (d　　　　　　) around the festival. Everybody is sticking to the rules, even the policemen. However, the co-founder of Extinction Rebellion doesn't think this is enough. She says the festival is a piece of (h　　　　　　), with a massive (f　　　　　　). People leave behind too much mess, even single-use tents. She thinks the organisers should prevent that, too.

7 Follow Up

▶ **Discuss, write or present.**

1. What do you think about the new festival rules? Do Japanese music festivals and other events have similar rules?

2. Do you often buy plastic bottles, or do you carry your own bottle and refill it? Is there anything else that we can do to save resources and stop waste?

3. The co-founder of Extinction Rebellion said that the festival was a piece of hedonism, where we are not really looking at what we are doing. What do you think she meant? Is it OK to enjoy ourselves, do you think, or should we always be serious?

Unit 2

One Way to Find a Job

厳しい就職活動に直面して、まったく新しい切り口でアプローチした学生がいます。手応えはどうでしょうか。ニュースを見てみましょう。

Starting Off

1 Setting the Scene

▶ **What do you think?**

1. What sort of job do you do, or would like to do in the future?
2. What sort of things do you have to do if you want someone to give you a good job?
3. What sort of person do you think employers are looking for?

2 Building Language

▶ **Which word or phrase (1-6) best fits which explanation (a-f)?**

1. placement [ ]
2. rejection [ ]
3. tenacity [ ]
4. fierce [ ]
5. stand out [ ]
6. succinct [ ]

a. be conspicuous, be easily noticed
b. the state of being refused, discarded, or thrown out
c. furious, intense, or strong
d. the quality of being persistent; refusal to give up
e. expressed clearly but briefly, in a few words
f. a position of employment, sometimes unpaid

Watching the News

3 Understanding Check 1

▶ Read the quotes, then watch the news and match them to the right people.

1. ... I decided that I was going to take matters into my own hands ... [   ]

2. Getting a job, or even work experience in London can be very competitive ... [   ]

3. I'll share it everywhere. [   ]

4. And I think that's also the challenge, you know ... [   ]

4 Understanding Check 2

▶ Which is the best answer?

1. Why does Josue Bapeck think that outside a tube station is a good place to look for a work placement?
   a. He can meet people in management consulting.
   b. He can speak to people while he is waiting for a train.
   c. He thinks it is a good place to get noticed.
   d. He can ask people what they think about their jobs.

2. What does Josue Bapeck think that a lot of employers are looking for?
   a. He thinks they are looking for somebody who has excellent qualifications.
   b. He thinks they are looking for an intelligent person.
   c. He thinks they are looking for an experienced person.
   d. He thinks they are looking for somebody who is tenacious.

3. What example does Josue Bapeck give of his experience at the station being really positive?
   a. He was given lunch and a hug.
   b. Lots of people took his photograph.
   c. Somebody offered him a job.
   d. Lots of people have viewed him on Instagram and LinkedIn.

4. What is Josue Bapeck studying, and where?

_____

5. In the opinion of the first man (in the blue jacket), what is the challenge?

_____

6. How did the second man know Josue Bapeck?

_____

BACKGROUND INFORMATION

イギリスの大学は3年制が一般的で、多くの学生は卒業後に就職活動を始めます。イギリスで2014年に大学を卒業した人の数は33万8,230人でした。翌2015年には31万2,330人に減少しましたが、2016年は31万6,690人、2017年は32万9,325人と、やや増加しました。2017年の大卒者のうち25万4,495人が回答した調査の結果によると、卒業後6ヶ月以内に就職した人は74.3％でした。その内訳は、国内のフルタイムの仕事に就いた人が55.2％、国内でのパートタイムが11.9％、進学し学業と仕事を併行する人が5.4％、海外で就職した人が1.8％でした。また、卒業後6ヶ月以内に職に就かなかった大卒者の割合は、2014年には6.3％でしたが、その後は減少し、2017年は5.1％に留まりました。2016年の国民投票でイギリスのEU離脱が決まったことで、雇用や経済への打撃が懸念されてきましたが、大卒の労働市場においては大きな変化は見られていません。しかし、2020年のEUからの正式な離脱と、新型コロナウイルスの流行により、今後様々な影響が出てくることが予想されています。

希望の仕事に就くにはどのようなことをすればよいのでしょうか。イギリスでは、採用選考にあたって職業経験や資格・技能が重視されます。そのため、今回のニュースに出てきた大学生のように、在学中や卒業後にインターンシップやボランティアなどに参加して、自分が就職したい分野の仕事をあらかじめ経験しておくことが大切です。こうした経歴や自分の適性を企業に向けてアピールすべく、近年ではソーシャルメディアを取り入れての就職活動を行う人が増えています。例えば、ニュースでも触れられていた「リンクドイン（LinkedIn）」はビジネスに特化したソーシャルネットワークで、希望する業種についての情報の入手や、人脈づくりに活用することができます。企業の目に留まるような魅力的なプロフィールを作成するために、求職者たちは日々たくさんの経験を積み、色々な工夫を凝らしています。

参考：

https://luminate.prospects.ac.uk/what-do-graduates-do
https://www.prospects.ac.uk/careers-advice/getting-a-job/how-to-find-a-job

5 Filling Gaps | News Story

▶ **Watch the news, then fill the gaps in the text.**

Newsreader: Getting a job, or even work experience in London can be very competitive, but one university student from southeast London has taken a (¹   ) different approach, and it's ended up going viral. Josue Bapeck has been standing outside a busy (²   ) station holding a cardboard sign asking for a work (³

). Alistair Fee went to meet him.

Josue Bapeck: So, I'm looking for work experience in management consulting, sales, or the tech (⁴   ).

First man: OK.

Alistair Fee: At London Bridge Station Josue isn't here to catch a train or a (⁵   ). He's here to get (⁶   ).

First man: Good to meet you.

Bapeck: Thank you. Nice to meet you.

First man: All the best, yeah.

Bapeck: I decided to come here because I had been applying for jobs online but I had been getting a lot of (⁷   ). And so I decided that I was going to take matters into my own hands, and show employers that I have (⁸   ), and enough (⁹   ) to stand outside here in London Bridge, where there are so many people looking at me, (¹⁰   ) me and lots of people walking past me, but I still have a (¹¹   ), and I think that that's something that a lot of employers are looking for.

First woman: I'll tag you. I'll share it everywhere. I love what you're doing.

Fec: And it's working. Hundreds have stopped.

First woman: I go to uni myself, and it's so hard to get experience without already being in the place. So to just do this, is such a good idea. You're going to get so many eyes on you, so, well done.

Fee: During a four-year electrical engineering course at the University of Southampton, he's looking for a (¹²   ) for the year ahead.

Bapeck: The com-, competition is (^{13}).
There-, I've got lots of graduates who have the same skills as me, going for the same jobs so I thought that it would be a good idea to make myself (^{14}) (^{15}) anyway that I could.

Fee: By encouraging photos, he's gone viral.

First man: And it takes (^{16}) to stand like he's doing there, you know and, and saying, "Here I am. Ah, this is my story." And I think that's also the challenge, you know, one has to learn how to tell your story in a (^{17}), clear way.

Fee: His picture's been seen a million times on Twitter. Tens of thousands have (^{18}) him on Instagram and LinkedIn.

Fee: Do you know Josue?

Second man: Yeah, I do. We went to the same school actually.

Fee: What do you think of what he's up to here?

Second man: Yeah, I think it's alright.

Fee: Do you think it's a brave move?

Third man: Yeah, 100%. Yeah, yeah, it takes a lot of, um, (^{19}) to do that, I think, especially in the middle of London.

Fee: After several days, he's something of a (^{20}) here.

Second woman: I think he just needs help. And there's not enough (^{21}) now going on, and I think this is the only way he thinks that he can, somebody can help him, and I think it's a very, very good idea. Very, very good idea.

Fee: You work here. Have you seen anybody else doing something at this station?

Second woman: No. No, I haven't, haven't seen anyone!

Bapeck: It's just been really, really (^{22}). On the first day, in fact, someone even (^{23}) me lunch. Then one lady gave me a big hug. So it's been very (^{24}).

Fee: Alistair Fee, BBC London.

(Thursday 10 October 2019)

Notes

l.12 **London Bridge Station**「ロンドン・ブリッジ駅」ロンドンの主要駅の1つ。地下鉄ノーザンライン と接続し、ブライトン方面へ運行している　l.30 **the University of Southampton**「サウサンプトン大 学」イングランド南部のハンプシャーにある大学

BEHIND THE SCENES

自分探しをするためのギャップイヤー

イギリスには、高校や大学を卒業後、すぐに進学や就職をせずに1年間程度休暇を取る「ギャップイヤー (gap year)」という制度があります。学生はこの期間に、インターンシップ、ボランティア活動、世界一周旅行、留学や起業などを行って、やりたい事を見つけたり、新しい事に挑戦したり、異なる文化に触れたりした上で、次のステップに進みます。例えばウィリアム王子 (Prince William, 1982-) は、高校卒業後のギャップイヤー中に、「ローリー・インターナショナル (Raleigh International)」という持続可能な開発に関わる慈善団体の国際的な若者育成プロジェクトに参加しました。こうしたブランクは、経歴上の支障になるどころか、社会全体によって推奨されており、日本の大学でもギャップイヤーを取り入れつつあります。

Moving On

6 Making a Summary

CD1-07

▶ Fill the gaps to complete the summary.

Josue Bapeck is studying electrical engineering at university, and is looking for a (p　　　　　　) for the year ahead. However, he has been applying online, and getting lots of (r　　　　　　). So he decided to stand outside London Bridge Station with a sign introducing himself and what he was looking for. He thinks that this proves he has (t　　　　　　), which he thinks is what employers are looking for. The competition is (f　　　　　　) so he wants to make himself (s　　　　　　) (o　　　　　　) any way he can. According to one man, what Josue is doing takes courage, but the challenge is being able to tell his story in a (s　　　　　　) way. Lots of other passers-by, including one man from the same school as Josue, think it is a good idea, too. Josue himself says the experience has been really positive, as he has received a free lunch and a big hug.

7 Follow Up

▶ Discuss, write or present.

1. What do you think of Josue Bapeck's idea? Would you be able to do that?
2. What do you think possible employers would think of Josue? Do you agree that employers are looking for tenacity? Is this a good way to show tenacity?
3. How do you think the internet has affected job-hunting in the past twenty years?

Unit 3

Sport for Musicians

オーケストラの若い演奏家たちを、少し変わったコーチが指導しています。どのようなレッスンが行われているのでしょうか。ニュースを見てみましょう。

Starting Off

1 Setting the Scene

▶ **What do you think?**

1. Do you play a musical instrument, or know somebody who does? How difficult do you think it is to perform well? What are the biggest difficulties?

2. Do you play any sports? What do you think sportsmen or sportswomen are thinking when they are trying to do their best?

3. What similarities do you think there are between playing a sport well and playing music well?

2 Building Language

▶ **Which word (1-5) best fits which explanation (a-e)?**

1. overlap   [   ]   **a.** successfully handle a difficult situation
2. fundamental [   ]   **b.** connect, share certain features
3. strive   [   ]   **c.** most basic or essential
4. cope   [   ]   **d.** try very hard
5. struggle   [   ]   **e.** experience difficulties

Watching the News

3 Understanding Check 1

▶ **Read the quotes, then watch the news and match them to the right people.**

1. It was a really good opportunity to share with each other ... [ ]

2. ... we'll move on to the world of sport, and the world of music. [ ]

3. ... I'm really grateful that Claire enabled me to think like that. [ ]

4. ... you might have someone in a concert hall ... [ ]

4 Understanding Check 2

▶ **Which is the best answer?**

1. According to the video, what do athletes and musicians have in common?
   a. They both find it impossible to perform under pressure.
   b. They both perform better when they are under pressure.
   c. They both try to perform perfectly under pressure.
   d. Neither can give a perfect performance unless they are under pressure.

2. What were the two lessons learnt by the musicians?
   a. Try to forget your concerns, and don't think of anything except now.
   b. Think about your concerns, and talk only about now.
   c. Talk about your concerns, and try not to think about now.
   d. Talk about your concerns, and think only about now.

3. Where are these musicians going next?
   a. to the next stage in their careers
   b. to the next stage for their performance
   c. to take a test about their sporting knowledge
   d. to an important concert, where they will perform perfectly

▶ **What do you remember?**

4. What is Claire Bennett, the performance coach, teaching the musicians?

_____

5. How did the teaching help the trumpeter?

_____

6. After lessons with Claire, how does the flautist feel about music?

_____

BACKGROUND INFORMATION

　今回のニュースは、ストレスの多い場面でメンタルの強さを発揮するというスポーツ心理学が、音楽の世界でも活かされるという話題でした。スポーツ心理学の歴史は、1898年、アメリカの心理学者ノーマン・トリプレット（Norman Triplett, 1861-1934）が、レース中の自転車競技者のほうが個人のタイムトライアル中の競技者よりも速く走行できると気づき、社会的影響がスポーツの結果の動機づけになる、と示したことに始まります。

　1925年にアメリカの心理学者コールマン・グリフィス（Coleman Griffith, 1893-1966）は、性格がスポーツの成果に与える影響を研究しました。彼は、プロのスポーツチームであるメジャーリーグのシカゴ・カブズ（Chicago Cubs）と初めて協働した心理学者でした。1960年代後半になり、アメリカン・フットボールのプロリーグであるNFLのいくつかのチームでヘッドコーチを務めたヴィンス・ロンバルディ（Vince Lombardi, 1913-70）は、選手たちの不安を取り除き、勝利だけが受け入れられる結果だと信じこませることで成功を収めました。1980年代には、アメリカのオリンピック委員会がスポーツ心理学の可能性に興味を持ちました。1983年、委員会は上級の学位を持つスポーツ心理学者を登録制にし、競技における心理面を向上させたいと願うアスリートに紹介しました。

　今日、メンタルの強さは、アスリート以外にも、エンターテイナー、ビジネスマン、軍事や医療従事者など、任務を遂行し成果を出さなくてはならない人々にとって、必要かつ有効な手段となっています。とりわけ、新型コロナウイルスの感染拡大で医療従事者のメンタルヘルスは重要な課題になっており、2020年4月、NHSイングランドは医療従事者を支援するための電話回線、メンタルヘルス・ホットラインを開設しました。

参考：
https://www.mentaltoughnessinc.com/history-of-mental-toughness/
https://www.bbc.com/news/uk-52702048

▶ **Watch the news, then fill the gaps in the text.**

Newsreader: Now, we'll move on to the world of sport, and the world of music. You might think the two don't (¹   ) but listen to this first because athletes and musicians are both (²   ) to perform at their best under (³   ), so a gold medal winning fencer thought her story could help an (⁴   ). The result: she was right. Here's Emma Jones.

Emma Jones: Some fine-tuning (⁵   ) of their final performances: a Southbank Sinfonia 2019. And watching on, someone hoping these young musicians are feeling a little happier and more (⁶   ) after learning some of the tools and (⁷   ) that helped her as a fencer.

Claire Bennett, former fencer: The (⁸   ) are, are just, you know, are, are fascinating. Um, you know, on the one hand, you might have someone in a concert hall, or you've got an athlete on a pitch, you've got someone holding a violin, or holding a rugby ball, um, but the (⁹   ) thing that kind of brings us together is the fact that, um, we're kind of (¹⁰   ) for that perfect performance.

Jones: Claire Bennett was an (¹¹   ) fencer. Now, as a performance coach, she teaches others how to (¹²   ) with the pressures of being their best at the highest level. One lesson taught and learnt: talk about your (¹³   ).

Erika Curbelo, trumpeter: It was a really good opportunity to share with each other, what we (¹⁴   ) with, what our fears were, what our (¹⁵   ) were, er, about performances to come. And sharing our sort of (¹⁶   ) helped a lot in kind of helping each other out.

Jones: Another lesson learnt: don't think about anything but (¹⁷   ).

Jack Welch, flautist: I try and really flick that switch and be in the moment. And I (¹⁸   ) enjoy music making so much more. And it's so much more fun, which is so (¹⁹   ). Um, yeah, and I'm, I'm really grateful that Claire enabled me to think like that.

35

Jones: These musicians are now moving on to the next stage in their (²⁰   ), 40 with a bit of sporting knowledge to help them on their way. Emma Jones, BBC London.

(Thursday 28 November 2019)

Notes

l.10 **Southbank Sinfonia**「サウスバンク・シンフォニア」ロンドンに拠点を持つイギリスの交響楽団。大卒の若手の演奏家の育成に力を入れており、毎年33人の研修生を受け入れている。今回のニュースに登場しているのは2019年度のメンバー。2002年設立　l.13 **Claire Bennett**「クレア・ベネット」イギリスの元フェンシング選手。14歳から活躍を見せ、ヨーロッパや世界の数々の大会でイギリス代表を務めた。2012年の引退後は、若者の支援に尽力している　l.22 **performance coach**「パフォーマンス・コーチ」ビジネスなどにおいて、個人が実力を発揮しより良い成果を挙げられるように指導する人物のこと　l.41 **sporting knowledge**「スポーツの知識」sportには運動競技としての「スポーツ」という意味の他に「気晴らし」「楽しみ」という意味がある。ここでは、元スポーツ選手から学んだ知識と、演奏を楽しむという意味を掛け合わせている

> BEHIND THE SCENES

BBCプロムス

BBCプロムス（BBC Proms）は世界最大級の音楽祭で、クラシックを中心に、ジャズなど他分野も含む音楽会が連日開催され放映される、イギリスの夏の風物詩です。メイン会場は、ハイド・パークに隣接し5,272席を擁するロイヤル・アルバート・ホール（Royal Albert Hall）で、瀟洒なウィグモア・ホール（Wigmore Hall）もよく利用されます。最終日は9月の第2土曜日で、「プロムス最終夜（The Last Night of the Proms）」と呼ばれ、ハイド・パークなどの公園に巨大なモニターが置かれ、人々は旗を振り、ピクニックを楽しみながらコンサートを鑑賞します。エドワード・エルガー（Sir Edward Elgar, 1857-1943）作曲の『威風堂々』（*Pomp and Circumstance*, 1902）や、第2の国歌とも言われ、ラグビー応援歌にも使われるウィリアム・ブレイク（William Blake, 1757-1827）作詞の賛美歌『エルサレム』（*Jerusalem*）が必ず演奏され、毎年熱狂のうちに幕を閉じます。

Moving On

6 Making a Summary

▶ Fill the gaps to complete the summary.

According to Claire Bennett, a former fencer, the world of music and the world of sport (o   ). Both musicians and athletes are under (p   ) to perform well, and the (f   ) thing is that they are both (s   ) to be perfect. She hopes that the techniques that helped her as a fencer will make the musicians feel happier and more confident, so that they can (c   ) with the (p   ). The musicians are learning to share about things they are (s   ) with, and their concerns for future performances. They also learn to think about the present moment. One musician said he was (g   ) to Claire for enabling him to enjoy his work much more. The musicians are now moving on to the next (s   ) in their careers.

7 Follow Up

▶ Discuss, write or present.

1. What do you think of the idea that you might cope better with pressures if you talk about and share your concerns? It seems to help in sport and music, but what about other areas of life and work?

2. What do you think is meant by not thinking of 'anything but now', and being 'in the moment'? Can you give some examples? How would it help musicians? What about other areas of life and work?

3. Whether you play sports or not, do you think that Claire Bennett's coaching would help you? Give some examples.

Unit 4

A Healthy Supermarket

イギリスでは人々の肥満が深刻な社会問題になっていますが、この問題を解決するためにロンドンのあるスーパーマーケットが画期的な試みを始めました。どのような取り組みなのでしょうか。ニュースを見てみましょう。

Starting Off

1 Setting the Scene

▶ **What do you think?**

1. Where do you (or your family) do your food shopping? Describe the shop. Where are all the different types of food placed in the shop?
2. What food do you buy every week?
3. If you want to be healthier, what sort of food should you buy? What sort of food should you avoid?

2 Building Language

▶ **For each word (1-5), find two synonyms (a-j).**

1. tempt   [   ] [   ]
2. tackle   [   ] [   ]
3. obesity   [   ] [   ]
4. treat   [   ] [   ]
5. overriding [   ] [   ]

a. overweight	**f.** fatness
b. fight	**g.** gift
c. predominant	**h.** major
d. delicacy	**i.** persuade
e. attack	**j.** attract

Watching the News

3 Understanding Check 1

▶ Read the quotes, then watch the news and match them to the right people.

1. Unhealthy products are part of our diet ...   [   ]

2. So, final thoughts, summary of your experience of this supermarket.   [   ]

3. More needs to be done by supermarkets ...   [   ]

4. And I feel like coming into somewhere like this. That would be a lot easier.   [   ]

4 Understanding Check 2

▶ Which is the best answer?

1. According to the video, how do shop layouts and special price offers affect customers?
   a. Customers might stay longer in the shop.
   b. They can encourage customers to buy unhealthy food.
   c. Customers are sometimes tempted to steal things.
   d. They might encourage customers to be careful about spending too much money.

2. In this pop-up shop, how is chocolate displayed differently?
   a. It is usually out of sight, but in this shop it is a staple food.
   b. In this shop, it takes a larger area because people like a treat.
   c. In this shop, chocolate is with the staple food, but in most shops, it is a treat.
   d. Usually, it is with the staple food, but in this shop it is out of sight.

3. What did Harry notice first?
   a. The fruit and vegetables are close to the entrance of the shop.
   b. The chocolate and snacks are right by the tills.
   c. The fruit and vegetables are positioned right by the tills.
   d. The bottles of water are much smaller.

4. What is the Royal Society of Public Health worried about, and why have they redesigned this store?

_____

5. What was the reaction of the British Retail Consortium?

_____

6. How did Harry summarise his experience of the supermarket?

_____

BACKGROUND INFORMATION

　肥満は、イギリスで深刻な社会問題となっています。2019年11月の発表では、最近20年間でイギリスの肥満人口はほぼ倍増し、イングランドでは人口の30％近い1,300万人に上っています。それに伴い、糖尿病、心臓病、癌などの生活習慣病や、膝の代替手術などが増加し、「国民保険サービス（National Health Service: NHS）」の財政を逼迫しています。そのため、病気の予防と健康で快適な生活がますます奨励されています。

　産業革命と、それに伴う公害などの負の側面を世界に先駆けて経験したイギリスでは、公衆衛生の概念も先駆的に打ち立てられました。今回スーパーマーケットの改革を手がけた「王立公衆衛生協会（The Royal Society of Public Health: RSPH）」は、公衆衛生の改善に尽力することを目的とする慈善団体で、公衆衛生に関する研究と啓蒙活動を行っています。女王の後援の下、2008年に「王立健康協会（The Royal Society of Health: RSH）」と「王立公衆衛生研究所（The Royal Institute of Public Health: RIPH）」が合併して設立されましたが、いずれも歴史のある協会で、イギリス最古の公衆衛生協会と認められています。協会は、政策、地域共同体、資格、訓練、認可事業などを通して、地域社会や個人が健康に暮らす支えとなっています。

　「スリミング・ワールド（Slimming World）」は、1969年にマーガレット・マイルズ・ブラムウェル（Margaret Miles-Bramwell, 1948- ）によって設立されたイギリスのダイエットクラブです。イングランド中部のダービーシャーが発祥ですが、今ではイギリス全土とアイルランドに広がっています。全ての年齢の男女に体重管理プログラムを提供し、教室やグループ活動を通して、理想体重の達成と維持をサポートし、同時にチャリティーも行っています。近年はSNSを活用し、半ばオンラインで交流を行い、互いの啓発を促しています。売り上げ優位の商業施設を消費者側が監督し、公衆衛生を改善する動きは、ますます活発になりそうです。

参考：
https://www.rsph.org.uk/about-us/history-of-rsph.html
https://www.slimmingworld.co.uk
https://www.theguardian.com/society/2019/nov/14/obesity-almost-doubles-in-20-years-to-affect-13-million-people

5 Filling Gaps | News Story

▶ **Watch the news, then fill the gaps in the text.**

Newsreader: More needs to be done by supermarkets to help (^{1}) (^{2}). That's according to a leading health charity who say shop layouts and cut-price offers often encourage us to be (^{3}) by the unhealthy options. The Royal Society of Public Health has (^{4}) a store in London to show how more healthy products can be (^{5}). Here's Tolu Adeoye.

Duncan Stephenson, Deputy Chief Executive of RSPH: So, the first thing you'll (^{6}) when you come in to the supermarket is we've (^{7}) the junk from the checkouts, and we've (^{8}) it with fruit and healthier snacks.

Tolu Adeoye: This is (^{9}) how all our supermarkets should look, to encourage us to eat better.

Stephenson: We've moved the unhealthier products to the bottom shelves so you can see here, the sugary ce-, cereals are still (^{10}), but they're positioned out of eyesight.

Adeoye: The pop-up has been set up by the Royal Society of Public Health, and the weight-loss organisation, Slimming World.

Stephenson: We still have chocolate here, chocolate cakes and biscuits but it's a much smaller area and it is out of sight, but we (^{11}) people like a (^{12}).

Adeoye: They say more traditional supermarket layouts are making us fat and must be (^{13}).

Stephenson: Unhealthy products are part of our diet, but they should be (^{14}) as a (^{15}) and not the main (^{16}). And if you look at the mo-, most supermarket layouts, it's as if they're part of the main (^{17}) of the diet.

Adeoye: But the British Retail Consortium says retailers have led the way when it comes to encouraging healthier eating. In a statement, it said, "Fresh fruit and vegetables are heavily price promoted and are often the first thing shoppers see when entering stores … where there is clear evidence specific proportional measures can help consumers the retail industry is open to Government action."

Adeoye: Back at the pop-up I meet Harry. He agrees to check out the layout.

Harry: Ah, it looks great. It looks great. I mean, firstly, the fact that all the fruit and veg is right by the tills, um, which I've not noticed before. Water is, is (**18**   ). And smaller bottles of anyth-, of, of high-sugar stuff. I don't see the chocolate. OK. I'm um, yeah, I don't know where it is.

Adeoye: Um …

Harry: OK.

Adeoye: Shall we go on a hunt?

Harry: Let's go on a hunt for some chocolate, yeah for sure. Or just for some sweet (**19**   ).

Adeoye: Yeah.

Harry: Yeah … oh, up there we go. Yeah, all good. I feel like it (**20**   ) the basics. You've got Tunnock's tea cakes in there, so I'm (**21**   ).

Adeoye: So, final thoughts, summary of your experience of this supermarket.

Harry: Um, I think the (**22**   ) thing is that it would, it would make me want to eat better, make better choices. I'm trying to think about what I'm eating, and where I'm buying things from. And I feel like coming into somewhere like this. That would be a lot easier.

Adeoye: The organisations behind the pop-up hope their ideas will be (**23**   ) (**24**   ) more widely. Tolu Adeoye, BBC London.

(Friday 26 July 2019)

Notes

l.7 **The Royal Society of Public Health**「王立公衆衛生協会」公衆衛生の改善に尽力することを目的とする慈善団体　l.19 **The pop-up (store)**「期間限定店」　l.20 **Slimming World**「スリミング・ワールド」イギリスの減量のためのダイエットクラブ。1969年設立　l.30 **the British Retail Consortium**「英国小売協会」イギリスの全小売業者のための商業組合。1992年設立　l.50 **Tunnock's**「タノックス」スコットランドに本社を置く家族経営の焼き菓子店。1890年設立

BEHIND THE SCENES

スーパーマーケットの発展

　スーパーマーケットの起源とされるのは、大量の商品を低価格で売る食料雑貨商（grocer）で、14世紀のロンドンにはすでに存在し、香辛料、紅茶、コーヒー、砂糖、小麦粉などの乾燥した食材を売っていたと言われています。商品の販売方法は今日見られるようなスーパーマーケットとは異なり、客がカウンター越しに店員に依頼して棚から商品を取ってもらい、代金を支払うという形式が長らく続いていました。しかし、1916年、アメリカの食料品店ピグリー・ウィグリー（Piggly Wiggly）が、客が自ら商品を手に取って選ぶことのできるセルフサービス形式を導入しました。以来、こうした販売方法が主流となっていき、より大型で幅広い商品を扱う店舗も見受けられるようになりました。現在では、セルフレジのみならず、アマゾンGo（Amazon Go）のようにレジすら存在しない店舗も登場しており、身近なスーパーマーケットの次なる進化が期待されています。

Moving On

6 Making a Summary

 CD1-13

▶ Fill the gaps to complete the summary.

　The Royal Society of Public Health is concerned about (o　　　　　　　), and wants to (t　　　　　　) it. It thinks that the layouts and cut-price offers of supermarkets (t　　　　　　) people to buy unhealthy food, and has redesigned a store to show how healthy products can be promoted. Near the checkouts of this store are fruit and healthy snacks, instead of junk food. The society understands that people like (t　　　　　　), but chocolate, cakes and biscuits are placed in a small area out of sight, instead of together with the (s　　　　　　) foods. One shopper, Harry, had to look for chocolate, but in the end he found some. He said that the (o　　　　　　) thing in this shop was that it would be easier to eat better and make better choices. Water is (k　　　　　　), and he noticed that fruit and vegetables were near the checkout. However, the British (R　　　　　　) Consortium pointed out that (r　　　　　　) promote healthy eating by promoting cheap fresh fruit and vegetables.

7 Follow Up

▶ Discuss, write or present.

1. Do you agree that the design of a supermarket can encourage you to buy healthy food? For example, if the chocolate and cakes were difficult to find would you buy less (or just look harder, like Harry?)

2. Obesity is a big problem in the UK. Why do you think so many people there are obese, and why is it a problem? Why doesn't Japan have the same problem?

3. What do you think is the biggest health problem in Japan, and how can we solve it?

Unit 5

Van Gogh's London House

ロンドンの一画に、オランダの画家ゴッホにゆかりのある家があります。その家に隠された歴史を紐解いてみましょう。

Starting Off

1 Setting the Scene

▶ **What do you think?**

1. What do you know about Vincent Van Gogh? Who was he, what did he do, and where did he live?
2. What is the oldest house or building you have ever been in? Where was it, and how old was it?
3. What toys do you think an English child would have played with in the 19th century?

2 Building Language

▶ **For each word (1-7), find two synonyms (a-n).**

1. restore   [   ] [   ]
2. launch   [   ] [   ]
3. spot   [   ] [   ]
4. funding   [   ] [   ]
5. fragment   [   ] [   ]
6. squirrel   [   ] [   ]
7. replicate [   ] [   ]

a. notice
b. part
c. piece
d. modernise
e. start
f. reproduce
g. open
h. finance
i. renovate
j. copy
k. see
l. save
m. support
n. hide

3 Understanding Check 1

▶ Read the quotes, then watch the news and match them to the right people.

1. Who's that, hmm? That's Mr. Vincent.

   [   ]

2. ... and anything that we could keep we've kept ...   [   ]

3. ... and has unexpectedly revealed secrets left hidden away for decades.

   [   ]

4. Good job he wasn't here to count the candles.   [   ]

a

b

c

d

4 Understanding Check 2

▶ Which is the best answer?

1. What are the actors doing in the Van Gogh House?
   a. They are restoring Van Gogh's House.
   b. They are looking for secrets.
   c. They are keeping the house open to the public.
   d. They are recreating the story of Van Gogh's time in London.

2. Which of the following was not found in the house?
   a. some sketches
   b. acorns
   c. insurance documents
   d. a praycr book

3. How is the Van Gogh House in London finding more money to pay for the work on the house?
   a. It has outside funding, and artists are also paying to work there.
   b. It has outside funding, and people are paying for special tours of the house.
   c. It doesn't have to pay anything. It's free.
   d. It has outside funding, and can sell documents they found in the house.

▶ **What do you remember?**

4. Who paid for the restoration of the house?

_____

5. In Livia Wang's opinion, why did James Wigmore have to hide his toys?

_____

6. What did Livia Wang's team do if they couldn't keep an original item in Van Gogh's House?

_____

BACKGROUND INFORMATION

　今回のニュースは、オランダの後期印象派の画家ヴィンセント・ヴァン・ゴッホ (Vincent Van Gogh, 1853-90) にまつわる家が、一般に公開されたという話題です。ロンドン、ストックウェルのハックフォード・ロード (Hackford Road)87番地にあるこの家は、2012年にオークションでジェームズ・ワン (James Wang) とアリス・チャイルズ (Alice Childs) 夫妻によって購入されました。このジョージ王朝時代のテラスハウスは、長年朽ちるに任されていましたが、この度7年間にわたる改装を経て2019年7月に開館し、ロンドンでのゴッホの生活を現代に伝えています。

　また、映像にも登場しますが、「ロンドン・ヴァン・ゴッホの家 (the Van Gogh House London)」には、ブルー・プラーク (blue plaque) というものが付けられています。ブルー・プラークとは、著名な人物がかつて住んだ家、もしくは歴史的な出来事があった場所に設置される直径50センチメートル程の青い銘板です。現在、ロンドン市内に900枚以上あるブルー・プラークですが、1867年に詩人ジョージ・ゴードン・バイロン卿 (Lord George Gordon Byron, 1788-1824) とイギリスに亡命したフランス皇帝ナポレオン3世 (Louis Napoleon Bonaparte, 1808-73) の住居に設置されたものが最初でした。当初は人文科学協会 (the Society of Arts) によって設置されましたが、1986年以降はイギリスの歴史的建造物や記念物を保存維持するための委員会であるイングリッシュ・ヘリテッジ (English Heritage) の管轄にあります。

　さらに、この建物はヒストリック・イングランド (Historic England) という団体によって、歴史的価値のある指定建造物 (Listed Buildings) として2級 (Grade II) に格付けされています。イングランドの指定建造物は1級、2*級、2級の3等級に分類され、約50万軒にのぼります。そのうち2級というのは特別な建造物に与えられ、指定建造物の91.7%を占めています。

　このようにゴッホの家は歴史の保護に努めていることはもちろん、次世代の芸術家や作家の支援にも尽力しており、過去と未来をつなぐ役割を果たしているのです。

参考：

https://www.vangoghhouse.co.uk
https://www.english-heritage.org.uk/visit/blue-plaques
https://historicengland.org.uk/listing/what-is-designation/listed-buildings/

5 Filling Gaps   **News Story**   ⊙ CD1-14 [Original] ⊙ CD1-15 [Voiced]

▶ **Watch the news, then fill the gaps in the text.**

Newsreader: Now the house where Vincent Van Gogh once lived in Stockwell has been (**1**   ) by a team of experts, and has unexpectedly revealed secrets left hidden away for decades. Now, for the first time, the house is being opened to the public. And to mark the (**2**   ),

the story of the artist's time here has been recreated by actors, as Victoria Cook went to see.

First actor: Who's that, hmm? That's Mr. Vincent.

Victoria Cook: The stories of Van Gogh's life in London, (**3**   ) (**4**   ) from his letters.

Second actor: Good job he wasn't here to count the candles.

Cook: Now the artist's former home's been (**5**   ), all (**6**   ) by a family based in London. During the works, a whole host of (**7**   ) treasures were found hidden away.

Livia Wang, Creative director, the Van Gogh House London: These are his landlady's (**8**   ) documents with all of her signatures on them, from the dates that he was living in this house. Um, and we also found this beautiful little (**9**   ) book, and all of this was folded up really neat-, neatly and hidden in the (**10**   ) upstairs.

Cook: Although Van Gogh lodged here for a year, he never (**11**   ) the loose floorboard in his bedroom.

Wang: So under this little floorboard we found (**12**   ) (**13**   ) Victorian children's toys, and what's really exciting is that they're all from pre-Van Gogh's time, in Van Gogh's bedroom. Um, so in here we found lots of acorns and marbles and little carved pigs and we also found sort of (**14**   ) of, um, handwriting samples that were all named and dated. So it's perfect, we could tell that it was this little boy called James Wigmore, who was 13, and had six younger brothers, and he lived in this house. So (**15**   ) he had to, to (**16**   ) everything away.

Cook: Amazing.

5

10

15

20

25

30

Cook: For Livia Wang this project's been a (¹⁷   ) of love.

Wang: We've had to do a lot of work really, and we've tried really, really hard to (¹⁸   ) all the original fabrics and anything that we could keep we've kept and anything that had to be changed, we've made a new one to try and (¹⁹   ) what was there before. And hopefully it'll (²⁰   ) for another 200 years.

Cook: Of course, none of this comes for (²¹   ). Outside (²²   ) being sought to keep the house running as an artist's space. That, and special (²³   ) of the house that the public can sign up for twice a week. Victoria Cook, BBC London, Stockwell.

(Saturday 27 July 2019)

Notes

l. 1 **Vincent Van Gogh**「ヴィンセント・ヴァン・ゴッホ（1853-90）」オランダの画家。代表作に『ひまわり』(Sunflowers, 1887)、『星月夜』(The Starry Night, 1889) などがある。画家を志す前、美術商であるグーピル商会の店員として、1873年から74年までをロンドンで過ごした　l. 2 **Stockwell**「ストックウェル」ロンドン南部のランベス自治区にある地域　l. 25 **Victorian**「ヴィクトリア朝時代の」ヴィクトリア女王（Queen Victoria, 1819-1901）の治世である1837年から1901年の、大英帝国の絶頂期とされる時代を指す

街中のアトラクション

アメリカ発祥のテーマパークは、広大な敷地にファンタジーの世界を体現していますが、ファンタジーの元祖とも言えるイギリスでは、一見匹敵するアトラクションがないように見えます。しかし、歴史的建造物が各地に点在するイギリスでは、シェイクスピアを生んだ演劇大国だけあり、観光地では歴史的衣装に身を包んだ役者が案内人を務め、小さなテーマを扱う博物館や、歴史的展示を含むアトラクションが街中にあります。例えばシェイクスピアの生誕地ストラトフォード・アポン・エイヴォン（Stratford-upon-Avon）では、母の生家から子孫の所有した家まで、シェイクスピアに関連する一連の建物の共通のチケットが販売されており、観光客はシェイクスピアの足跡を辿って町中を巡ります。実は、イギリスは、国全体をテーマパークのように捉えることもできるのです。

Moving On

6 Making a Summary

CD1-16

▶ Fill the gaps to complete the summary.

The house in London where Vincent Van Gogh stayed has been (r   ), (f   ) by a family, with some outside (f   ). It is being opened to the public, and the (l   ) is being marked by actors recreating his time in the house. A whole (h   ) of treasures were found, such as Van Gogh's landlady's insurance documents, and a beautiful little prayer book. Underneath a loose floorboard, which Van Gogh hadn't (s   ), they found acorns, marbles, and little carved pigs: toys which a young 13-year old boy had (s   ) away. There were also named and dated (f   ) of handwriting samples. In the (r   ) they tried hard to keep original items and fabrics, and if that wasn't possible, they (r   ) what was there before. The public can sign up for special tours twice a week, and it's hoped the house will last another 200 years.

7 Follow Up

▶ Discuss, write or present.

1. If you went to London, would you like to go on a special tour of Van Gogh's house? What would you be most interested in?

2. Do you know of any similar houses in Japan, where somebody famous lived? Can you describe them? What do they contain?

3. We have learnt about James Wigmore because he hid some of his belongings for us to find them 200 years later. If you wanted people to learn about you in 200 years, what three things would you hide?

Unit **6**

Esports Scholarships

若者に人気のコンピューターゲーム。勉学の支障にならないか、親にとっては心配の種になることもありますが、アメリカではゲームの腕前で進学が決まることもあるようです。ニュースを見てみましょう。

▍ Starting Off

1 Setting the Scene

▶ **What do you think?**

1. How difficult is it to get a scholarship to a Japanese university? For what kind of subjects do Japanese universities usually grant scholarships?
2. What computer games do you know about? Do you or your friends play them competitively?
3. What sports do you enjoy watching? Why do you think so many people go to watch baseball, football or rugby games?

2 Building Language

▶ **Which word or phrase (1-5) best fits which explanation (a-e)?**

1. cover   [   ]   **a.** not trusting or believing; perhaps sarcastic
2. cynical   [   ]   **b.** supply with the necessary equipment
3. fit out   [   ]   **c.** include or deal with
4. cutthroat [   ]   **d.** harmonious, containing all the necessary ingredients
5. balanced   [   ]   **e.** ruthless, extremely competitive

3 Understanding Check 1

▶ Read the quotes, then watch the news and match them to the right people.

1. ... I don't know if I have that in me
    or, like, I want to do that.   [   ]

2. ... all the time you wasted in your
    bedroom was actually for something.
                                        [   ]

3. ... on your couch, eating doughnuts,
    and drinking diet coke.   [   ]

4. ... including some of the fastest
    computers.   [   ]

4 Understanding Check 2

▶ Which is the best answer?

1. Which of the following investments was <u>not</u> mentioned?
    a. millions of pounds for new headsets for college athletes
    b. a million-pound training facility
    c. a multi-million-dollar esports stadium
    d. 1.5 million pounds per year on coaching

2. Why is Harrisburg University so enthusiastic about esports?
    a. America needs more esports players.
    b. It is a good way for the university to make money.
    c. Game-playing skills should be encouraged for scientists of the future.
    d. Esports will help Harrisburg University become well-known.

3. What sort of change does Chris Buckler think will happen in the future?
    a. University teams will be all male.
    b. There will be females in the university esports team.
    c. People will be rewarded if they recognise 21st century sports stars.
    d. More universities will invest in esports.

4. Why was one esports student's mother relieved?

_____

5. What event happened in New York recently?

_____

6. According to Soames (the last student) what are the problems about being an esports professional?

_____

BACKGROUND INFORMATION

　近年注目されつつあるeスポーツの市場規模は2022年には約23億ドル（約2,500億円、1ドル＝107円）まで成長すると言われており、今や多くの大学が参入を始めています。2014年にロバート・モリス大学イリノイ校（Robert Morris University Illinois）がアメリカで初となるeスポーツ奨学金を導入して以来、メリービル大学（Maryville University）、カリフォルニア大学アーバイン校（University of California, Irvine）などが続々とeスポーツプログラムを開設しました。現在ではおよそ200の大学が年間約1,500万ドル（約16億円）をeスポーツの奨学金に投じており、平均で学生1人につき年間4,800ドル（約52万円）が付与されています。

　eスポーツを学ぶことで学位を取得できる大学も増えています。今回のニュースで取り上げられていたハリスバーグ大学は2018年にeスポーツ奨学金を開設し、満額の奨学金と住宅手当を選手たちに与えていますが、2020年には、新たにeスポーツマネジメントの課程を設置しました。ビジネスとしてのeスポーツを学ぶことができ、将来的にはコンテンツ制作やイベント企画、アナリストなどの職業への道が開けることが期待されています。イギリスでも、2018年にローハンプトン大学（University of Roehampton）が、国内で初めてeスポーツ奨学金を開設しました。また、スタッフォードシャー大学（Staffordshire University）も2018年よりeスポーツ課程を設置しており、大学スポーツや学問としてのeスポーツの地位が確立されつつあります。

　eスポーツ自体の人気にもますます拍車がかかっています。とりわけ2020年は、新型コロナウイルスの流行による外出規制のため、自宅でオンラインゲームを楽しむ人が急増しました。また、従来型のスポーツイベントが取りやめになる中、メジャーリーガーや自動車レーサー、バスケットボール選手など、プロのアスリートたちが続々とeスポーツに参戦したことで、新たなファン層の獲得も進んでいます。学生や若者だけでなく、様々な世代を取り込んで、eスポーツ界はさらなる盛り上がりを見せています。

参考：
https://nacesports.org/what-is-e-sports/
https://harrisburgu.edu/
https://www.staffs.ac.uk/course/esports-ba

5 Filling Gaps   News Story   ⊙ CD1-17 [Original] ⊙ CD1-18 [Voiced]

▶ **Watch the news, then fill the gaps in the text.**

Newsreader: Now, games consoles are once again at the top of many Christmas present lists, of course. A lot of parents will angst that this is all a horrible (¹   ) of time, of course, but in the United States now, playing esports can actually be a way into university because some colleges are (²   ) championships, and the best players get offered full scholarships. Here's our North America correspondent, Chris Buckler.

5

Chris Buckler: You'll find the newest college (³   ) not in helmets, but in headsets.   10

Coach: So I'm sitting here with Soames, one of the Overwatch players at Harrisburg University. Um, and he's (⁴   ) playing, er, Overwatch, er, which is a competitive, team-based game.

Buckler: Coaches at this Pennsylvania college watch every (⁵   ) of the   15 keyboard and move of the mouse.

Buckler: Meet the (⁶   ) competitive esport (⁷   ) on full university scholarships.

Hunter Rogers, student: My mum ... it was kind of like, a sigh of relief 'cos, she was able to go like, "Wow, all the time you wasted in your bedroom was actually for   20 something."

Buckler: Some might be (⁸   ), but this is being presented as the latest university team sport. This year's collegiate tournament was even (⁹   ) by the leading US sports network, ESPN.

Buckler: It cost the (¹⁰   ) of a million pounds, building this training   25 facility, and (¹¹   ) (¹²   ) (¹³   ) with some of the best (¹⁴   ), including some of the fastest computers. And Harrisburg University is spending another one-and-a-half million pounds every year on coaching its teams, and providing scholarships. This is a big (¹⁵   ) for the college.

30

Eric Darr, President, Harrisburg University:
Competitive video gaming that we have at Harrisburg University is night and day different than (**16**   ) gaming on your couch, eating doughnuts, and drinking diet coke. That, this is not that.

Buckler: Harrisburg is an old (**17**   ) city, but its young university is focused on the future, and it believes it can use gaming to get noticed as interest grows across America. Nearby in Philadelphia a multi-million-dollar esports (**18**   ) is being built. It will host tournaments like the recent competition in New York, that attracted huge crowds, to watch people playing the game Fortnite. It was (**19**   ) online all over the world and there was big prize money. 40

Soames Lovett-Darby, student: It's like ... a professional at the top level, it's very (**20**   ), and you need to play like 10, 11, 12 hours a day. Um, and I don't know if I have that in me or, like, I want to do that. I'd rather have, like, a more (**21**   ) life. 45

Buckler: One thing striking about this university team is it's all male. But that is likely to change, if players are recognised and rewarded as 21st century sports stars. Chris Buckler, BBC News, Harrisburg. 50

(Friday 13 December 2019)

Notes

l.12 **Harrisburg University**「ハリスバーグ大学」ペンシルヴァニア州ハリスバーグおよびフィラデルフィアにキャンパスを持つ理工系の私立大学　l.12 **Overwatch**「オーバーウォッチ」2016年5月にブリザード・エンターテイメントより発売されたアクションシューティングゲーム　l.24 **ESPN** 全米にネットワークを持つスポーツ中心のケーブルテレビ局。1979年にコネチカット州ブリストルで開局。元々はEntertainment and Sports Programming Network の頭文字を取ったもの　l.40 **Philadelphia**「フィラデルフィア」ペンシルヴァニア州最大の都市　l.43 **Fortnite**「フォートナイト」2017年7月にエピック・ゲームズより発売されたアクションビルディングゲーム

BEHIND THE SCENES

オリンピックを目指すeスポーツ

　eスポーツの歴史は、1972年10月、アメリカのスタンフォード大学で「スペースウォー(Spacewar)」というゲームの大会が行われたことに遡ります。1997年5月には最初のプロの競技会が行われ、同年6月には最初のプロリーグ「サイバーアスリート・プロフェッショナル・リーグ(Cyberathlete Professional League)」が誕生しました。その後、参加者と会場の規模は拡大を続け、勝者への賞金は100万ドルを超える額になりました。このような状況で、eスポーツの世界大会を求める声が高まり、2018年にはインドネシアのジャカルタで行われたアジア競技大会において参考競技としてeスポーツが行われました。しかし、プレイするゲームの選定やゲーム制作企業の著作権などの問題があり、いまだにオリンピック競技には認められていません。

Moving On

6 Making a Summary

▶ Fill the gaps to complete the summary.

　(C   ) people might think that computer games are a waste of time, but some American universities are now (h   ) esports championships, and the best players are even offered scholarships. However, unlike casual gaming, these championships are (f   ) competitive, involve lots of money, and are even (c   ) by major television networks. A recent competition in New York attracted huge crowds. Hoping it will get noticed, Harrisburg University spent a million pounds (f   ) (o   ) a training facility with the best equipment, and will spend 1.5 million pounds a year on gaming coaching and scholarships. However, the (c   ) competition might not suit everyone, and one team player said he would prefer a more (b   ) life to having to play 12 hours a day.

7 Follow Up

▶ Discuss, write or present.

1. What do you think about universities giving scholarships to people who are good at esports? Do you think it is fair?

2. Harrisburg is spending one-and-a-half million pounds every year on esports. Do you think this is a good investment? Is there anything else that you think they should invest in?

3. At the end, Soames Lovett-Darby said he would rather have a more balanced life. What do you think he means? Do you think you have a balanced life? If not, what is missing?

36

Unit 7

Snow-Camp

イギリスはチャリティーが盛んですが、BBC のチルドレン・イン・ニードという活動も、その一端を担っています。寄付金の用途を追ってみましょう。

Starting Off

1 Setting the Scene

▶ **What do you think?**

1. What sports do you like, or would you like to try? Why?
2. Are there any ways in which playing a sport might have changed you? For example, if you played one, did it make you a better person?
3. What about winter sports? Do you think there is anything special about winter sports?

2 Building Language

▶ **Which word (1-5) best fits which explanation (a-e)?**

1. donation   [   ]   **a.** strong enthusiasm for something
2. passion   [   ]   **b.** very big, enormous
3. massive   [   ]   **c.** a gift, usually to a charity or a good cause
4. drift   [   ]   **d.** something to worry about or a challenge to be met
5. issue   [   ]   **e.** move without purpose or accidentally from place to place

3 Understanding Check 1

▶ **Read the quotes, then watch the news and match them to the right people.**

1. We all started somewhere.   [   ]

2. A little, yeah. But it, it's fine.   [   ]

3. But for Londoners like Laquan this is about so much more than skiing.
   [   ]

4. All you want to do from here is start to bring those skis nice and straight.
   [   ]

4 Understanding Check 2

▶ **Which is the best answer?**

1. What does the organisation 'Snow-Camp' do?
   a. It helps poor children by introducing them to winter sports.
   b. It raises millions of pounds for Children in Need.
   c. It spends money from donations on improving ski areas in Britain.
   d. It trains young skiers who are good enough to win competitions.

2. When did Laquan start skiing?
   a. after he graduated from school
   b. four years before this video was aired
   c. when he was 18
   d. after he had got into lots of trouble as a teenager

3. At the end of the video, Laquan tells us how Snow-Camp has helped him. What did he <u>not</u> mention?
   a. He has discovered what he wants to do.
   b. It has enabled him to make himself a better person.
   c. It has helped him to find a good job.
   d. He has learnt things about himself that he didn't know before.

▶ **What do you remember?**

4. Why was it difficult for Laquan growing up around Pimlico?

_____

5. The Snow-Camp charity is not just about learning to ski. What is it also about?

_____

6. What did 18-year-old Zulika say about the young people starting on the Snow-Camp programme?

_____

BACKGROUND INFORMATION

　BBCが主催する「チルドレン・イン・ニード（Children in Need）」は、イギリス国内を中心として恵まれない子供や若者を支援する活動を行っています。発端は1927年のクリスマスにBBCがラジオで呼びかけた子供のための募金で、現在の70,000ポンド（約980万円）に相当する金額が集まり、複数の慈善団体に寄付されました。その後も様々な形で活動が続けられ、1980年には「チルドレン・イン・ニード」として初の長時間テレビ番組が放送され、100万ポンド（約1億4,000万円）の寄付金が集まりました。現在までに総額10億万ポンド（約1,400億万円）を超える寄付金が集められ、子供や若者への支援に用いられています。

　2019年、チルドレン・イン・ニードは10万ポンド（約1,400万円）を「スノー・キャンプ（Snow-Camp）」に寄付しました。スノー・キャンプは2003年に設立された団体で、貧困にあえぎ犯罪が多発する地域出身の若者たちにスキーやスノーボードなどのスポーツに触れる機会を提供し、前向きに生活していくためのスキルを教えています。現在では年間1,000人の若者をプログラムを通じて支援していますが、今回の寄付金により、150人のロンドンの若者がプログラムに参加することが可能となりました。若者たちはスキーやスノーボードを実際に体験するところから始めて、イングランドのスノースポーツインストラクター1級の資格を得るための訓練を受け、資格取得や生活スキルの向上のための講座を受講します。こうした活動の成果により、これまでの参加者の98パーセントは自分に自信を持つことができるようになったと感じ、91パーセントはスノースポーツやその他の業界で職を得たり、進学の道を選んだりなど、人生を前向きに進んでいます。

参考：

https://www.bbcchildreninneed.co.uk/
https://www.snow-camp.org.uk/

5 Filling Gaps

News Story

CD1-20 [Original] CD1-21 [Voiced]

▶ Watch the news, then fill the gaps in the text.

Newsreader: Now every year your (¹ _____) help raise millions for Children in Need and this week we want to show you how some of that money is spent. Today, we're featuring the work of Snow-Camp, which supports children from (² _____) communities through skiing. Riz Lateef has the story. 5

Riz Lateef: A (³ _____) for the slopes and showing off his moves at the Snow Centre in Hemel Hempstead. But for Londoners like Laquan this is about so much more than skiing. 10

Laquan: Growing up around Pimlico, um, for role models it was quite hard. There was no one that was trying to make kind of like a (⁴ _____), positive impact on the young people. And there was a lot of (⁵ _____), eh, daily (⁶ _____) that you get every day: arrests, um, fights, things like that.

Lateef: So could you have (⁷ _____) into things you shouldn't have? 15

Laquan: Um, I would say yeah, very easily. There was a lot of times where I even thought to myself like, "Oh, let's go with them and get (⁸ _____)".

Lateef: And for you, Snow-Camp came along.

Laquan: Yeah, they kind of changed, my whole kind of (⁹ _____) on life. Coming from inner city kind of London, Pimlico, I didn't expect ev-, ever to have 20 this sort of (¹⁰ _____) handed to me.

Laquan: OK, make sure you (¹¹ _____) on those inside (¹² _____). All you want to do from here is start to bring those skis nice and straight.

Lateef: From first (¹³ _____) on the snow four years ago, Laquan is now a qualified instructor. But the charity's work is also about (¹⁴ _____) with 25 young people through skiing and snowboarding, and helping them develop (¹⁵ _____) life skills.

Laquan: Really well done. Really good.

Lateef: These teenagers from across London are getting a chance to try out the slopes. 30

Lateef: Were you scared at all?

Girl: A little, yeah. But it, it's fine.

Boy: It's really good, like you should try it.

Zulika: Careful of the (¹⁶   ), they are quite sharp.

Lateef: Well, someone who tried it, and loved it, is 18-year-old Zulika, who went through the Snow-Camp (¹⁷   ) and now helps out. She knows only too well how they're feeling.

Zulika: We all started somewhere. We all, no one knew how to ski, we all came here with the same question of "Am I gonna be able to do this?" "Am I gonna get it?" "Am I gonna get the hang of it?"

Lateef: Thanks to (¹⁸   ) from Children in Need, more young people from inner city areas will get the chance to take part in these (¹⁹   ), and perhaps help change their lives, like Laquan.

Laquan: Snow-Camp has helped me to kind of find myself. Um, they helped me to learn things about myself I didn't know myself. And now that I know I can kind of help to (²⁰   ) on them and make myself a (²¹   ) person. They've just helped me to kind of (²²   ) what I wanted to do and who I want to be.

(Wednesday 13 November 2019)

Notes

l.3 **Children in Need**「チルドレン・イン・ニード」1980 年以来 BBC が主催するチャリティーイベントで、放送局が番組を通じて助けを必要とする子どもたちのための募金活動を行っている。11 月の金曜日に開催される　l.6 **Snow-Camp (Charity)**「スノー・キャンプ（チャリティー）」スキー・スノーボードの活動を通して、ロンドンの恵まれない地域の若者を支援する慈善団体　l.8 **the Snow Centre**「スノー・センター」イギリス最大の屋内スキー場　l.9 **Hemel Hempstead**「ヘメルヘムステッド」イングランド南東部ハートフォード州西部の町。ロンドンの北西にある　l.11 **Pimlico**「ピムリコー」ロンドン南西部の地区　l.20 **inner city**「都心」スラム化することが多い

BEHIND THE SCENES

有名な失敗ジャンパー

　スコットランドを除いて標高の高い雪山の少ないイギリスで、スキーは盛んなスポーツではありません。イギリス人がスキーをするには、ヨーロッパのアルプスなどに行かなくてはならず、そのためスキーは上流階級のスポーツと考えられています。過去の冬季オリンピックにおいて目立った活躍をした選手が少ない中、マイケル・エドワーズ（Michael Edwards, 1963- ）は、イギリス史上初のスキージャンプ代表として活躍しました。彼は1988年のカルガリー・冬季オリンピック（Calgary Winter Olympics）にイギリス唯一の代表選手として選ばれましたが、ジャンプに失敗すればするほど人気者になり、「エディー・ザ・イーグル（Eddie the Eagle）」のあだ名で愛されました。記録ではなく記憶に残るエドワーズの半生は『イーグル・ジャンプ』（*Eddie the Eagle*, 2016）という伝記映画になっています。

Moving On

6 Making a Summary

▶ **Fill the gaps to complete the summary.**

　　Children in Need is a charity that collects (d   ) and spends the money on programmes that support poor children from (d   ) communities. Snow-Camp is one such programme, which aims to connect with children through snow sports, and help them develop (k   ) life skills. Laquan joined Snow-Camp four years ago, and is now an instructor, with a (p   ) for the slopes. He grew up in Pimlico, where there were a lot of (i   ), like fights, and it was easy to (d   ) into doing things he shouldn't do. There were no role models, and nobody made any (m   ) positive impact on children. Then Snow-Camp came along and helped him to find himself and make himself a better person.

7 Follow Up

▶ **Discuss, write or present.**

1. Think about what these children do at Snow-Camp. The programme hopes to help them develop key life skills, and sometimes it changes their lives. But how do you think it does this? Why do you think it is so successful?

2. Laquan said Snow-Camp had helped him discover what he wanted to do, and who he wanted to be. What do you think he wants to do? What will happen to him in the future?

3. Children in Need supports children who are deprived, and need help in making themselves better people. They need donations. Would you donate to this charity? If so, why? Or are there other charities that you want to donate to?

Fighting Parkinson's with Ballet

一流のバレエ団がロンドンで特別なレッスンを開講しています。どのような人々が受講しているのでしょうか。ニュースを見てみましょう。

Starting Off

1 Setting the Scene

▶ **What do you think?**

1. What activities do you think are good for people who are sick?
2. Some diseases make it difficult for the sick person to move properly. Do you know what these diseases are, and perhaps do you know of anybody who has had such a disease?
3. Why do you think people have dancing lessons? What effect does dancing have on people?

2 Building Language

▶ **Which word or phrase (1-7) best fits which explanation (a-g)?**

1. symptom   [   ]   **a.** deliberate and voluntary; done with full awareness
2. neurological   [   ]   **b.** related to a person's nervous system
3. tremor   [   ]   **c.** able and eager to do something
4. stability   [   ]   **d.** a sign or indication, usually that something is wrong
5. conscious   [   ]   **e.** a shaking or vibrating movement, often involuntary
6. up for it   [   ]   **f.** strongly influenced by, or developed from, something
7. rooted in   [   ]   **g.** the ability to be steady, firm and balanced

3 Understanding Check 1

▶ Read the quotes, then watch the news and match them to the right people.

1. ... it's almost impossible to fight off the physical.   [   ]

2. And behind it all, is one of the UK's top ballet companies.   [   ]

3. ... so it's, it's a great class.   [   ]

4. ... I skip down the road as though I'm pretending to be Margot Fontaine.   [   ]

4 Understanding Check 2

▶ Which is the best answer?

1. Why are these people taking ballet classes?
   a. They have Parkinson's and need help in dealing with the symptoms.
   b. They think that ballet can help prevent Parkinson's.
   c. They think that ballet can cure Parkinson's.
   d. They want to be good ballet dancers.

2. Which of the following is not a symptom of Parkinson's?
   a. instability
   b. a tremor
   c. loss of hearing
   d. difficulty in stretching limbs

3. Which sentence best describes the attitude of the second man?
   a. Crossing the mental barrier is the easiest challenge.
   b. If you are in bad physical shape, it's impossible to improve your mental state.
   c. If you can't give it your best, then you should give in.
   d. It is really important to be motivated.

4. What did the first man say about the ballet lessons?

_____

5. When people are learning to dance, what happens to their brains?

_____

6. According to the ballet teacher, how do her lessons change the students?

_____

BACKGROUND INFORMATION

　パーキンソン病とは、震え、動作緩慢、筋肉の強張り、体のバランスが崩れ転びやすくなる姿勢保持障害を主な症状とする病気です。主に50代以上で起こる病気ですが、40代以下で起こる場合もあり、若年性パーキンソン病と呼ばれます。原因となる特別な理由はわかっていませんが、大脳の下にある中脳の黒質ドーパミン神経細胞が減少することで起こります。完治する治療法が確立されていない難病ですが、進行性の病であり、進行を遅らせる処置はできます。また、便秘や頻尿、発汗、疲れやすさ、嗅覚の低下、立ちくらみ、うつ、興味が薄れたり意欲が低下したりする、などの症状も起こることがあります。

　病気の進行を遅らせる薬が研究開発され、現在のパーキンソン病患者の平均寿命は全体の平均とほとんど変わらないと考えられています。運動、睡眠、食事、薬が基本とされ、転倒や誤飲によって他の病気を引き起こさないように気をつけながら、激しい運動ではなく、散歩やストレッチなど、適度な運動を続けることが奨励されています。

　高齢になる程発症率の高くなるパーキンソン病ですが、若年で発症した患者の中には、診断が遅れたり、差別や偏見に苦しんだりする例も見られ、また病気への誤解から悩みを抱える患者も少なくありません。患者も社会も、パーキンソン病を正しく理解し、対処する必要があります。

　人口の高齢化に伴い、イギリスのパーキンソン病患者数は増加の傾向にあり、2018年には350人に1人にあたる約145,000人の患者がいました。患者をサポートする団体である「パーキンソンズUK (Parkinson's UK)」は、病気に関する最新情報を提供したり、地域ごとに日常のサポートを提供したりしています。落ち込みがちな精神面を支えながら適度な運動を促す活動が行われており、ニュースで紹介されているバレエ以外にも、タンゴやヨガ、ピラティスなど様々なクラスや交流の場が設けられています。

参考：
https://www.parkinson.org/understanding-parkinsons/what-is-parkinsons
https://www.bbc.com/news/uk-northern-ireland-foyle-west-49883137
https://www.bbc.com/news/health-48691633

5 Filling Gaps — News Story

CD1-23 [Original] · CD1-24 [Voiced]

▶ **Watch the news, then fill the gaps in the text.**

Newsreader: They say it's like being given a new lease of life: taking ballet classes to help with the (¹   ) of Parkinson's. Londoners tell us it's helping with (²   ) and a sense of (³   ). And behind it all, is one of the UK's top ballet companies. Alice Bhandhukravi has the story.

Kate Hartley-Stevens, the English National Ballet: Here we go and plié, stretch, rise up ...

Alice Bhandhukravi: Though it may look like a gentle warm-up, in fact what is happening in this ballet class at the Royal Albert Hall is something quite important. The (⁴   ) here have Parkinson's, a (⁵   ) condition which gets worse over time. As well as the more obvious (⁶   ), it means sufferers can struggle to stretch their limbs, and (⁷   ) can be a serious challenge. But with the help of dancers from the English National Ballet, these people with Parkinson's are learning to move again.

Alan Ferrett, Ambassador, Dance for Parkinson's: It's like being in a home because you can relax, you can be yourself, you're with other people that are shaking, or that can't hardly move. I can totally be myself and not (⁸   ).

Bhandhukravi: At the University of Roehampton, they've been studying the physical, social and emotional (⁹   ) of this class, and the benefits of ballet have been (¹⁰   ) proven. It seems when dancing, the brain is being (¹¹   ) retrained to make certain movements. It's certainly working for Sarah.

Sarah Beer, a participant: For me, I'm one of the more (¹²   ) people in a way that, so far as I can tell, the worst effects for me are the (¹³   ), and it is the depression and the anxiety, and after this, I, you know, I skip down the road as though I'm pretending to be Margot Fontaine.

Hartley-Stevens: 3-2-1 release!

Bhandhukravi: And for many people here, the ability to fight the physical battle against Parkinson's is (**14**   ) (**15**   ) the state of mind.

Guy Meredith, a participant: For me, it's a much more mental (**16**   ) that has to be crossed. You've got to fight it. You can't, can't give in. You know, you must give it, give it your best. If you are in a bad mental state, it's almost impossible to fight off the physical. So you've really got to make sure that you're really (**17**   ) (**18**   ) (**19**   ), you know.

Hartley-Stevens: They often seem to arrive perhaps a little stiff, a little bit (**20**   ) over, and then they leave, standing much taller, happier, more confident people to go out into the world, so it's, it's a great class.

Bhandhukravi: This is just one of the classes for people with Parkinson's. There are many more all over the capital. Alice Bhandhukravi, BBC London News.

(Tuesday 2 April 2019)

Notes

l.4 **Parkinson's** (=Parkinson's disease)「パーキンソン病」手の震え、動作や歩行の困難などの運動障害を示す進行性の神経変性疾患　l.9 **the English National Ballet**「イングリッシュ・ナショナル・バレエ」ロンドン・コロシアム劇場を本拠地とするバレエ団。1950年設立　l.12 **the Royal Albert Hall**「ロイヤル・アルバート・ホール」イギリスのヴィクトリア女王(Queen Victoria, 1819-1901)の夫であるアルバート公(Prince Albert, 1819-61)に捧げられた演劇場。1871年開場　l.18 **Dance for Parkinson's**「ダンス・フォー・パーキンソンズ」世界25ヶ国、300以上の共同体において、パーキンソン病の患者に特別なダンス・レッスンを提供する団体。2001年設立　l.20 **that can't hardly** 文法的に正しくはthat can hardlyとなる　l.21 **the University of Roehampton**「ローハンプトン大学」ロンドンにある国立大学。1841年、前身となるホワイトランド・コレッジ設立　l.30 **Margot Fontaine**「マーゴ・フォンテイン(1919-91)」イギリスのバレエ・ダンサー。ロイヤル・バレエでプリマ・バレリーナとして活躍した

バレエの発展とフランス語

　「バレエ（ballet）」は、イタリア語で「踊る」を意味するballareから生じたフランス語です。15世紀のルネサンス期にイタリアの宮廷で始まったバレエは、16世紀、イタリアから嫁いだカトリーヌ・ド・メディシス（Catherine de Médicis, 1519-89）によってフランス王室にもたらされ、以後、バレエ好きのルイ14世（Louis XIV, 1638-1715）の時代を経て大きく発展しました。現在見られるバレエ用語の多くはフランス語です。バレリーナが履くトウシューズを英語ではpointe shoesと呼びますが、「ポワント」は「つま先立ち」を意味する用語です。また、スカート状の衣装であるチュチュ（tutu）は、フランス語の幼児語で「お尻」を意味するcucuに由来するとされています。

Moving On

6 Making a Summary

CD1-25

▶ Fill the gaps to complete the summary.

　Parkinson's is a (n　　　　　　　) disease which gets worse over time. There is no cure, but we try to improve the (s　　　　　　　). The most noticeable (s　　　　　　) is a (t　　　　　　), and sufferers find it difficult to stretch their limbs, and keep their (s　　　　　　). Some Londoners with Parkinson's think that ballet classes can help them. They say it allows them to be themselves, and their teacher notices that after a class they are much happier and more self-confident. It has been proven that dancing (c　　　　　　) retrains the mind to make certain movements, and many people think that the ability to fight against Parkinson's is in fact (r　　　　　　) in the mind. One student said it was important to cross the mental (b　　　　　　), and to benefit from the dancing lessons you must make sure you're really (u　　　　　　) (f　　　　　　) (i　　　　　　).

7 Follow Up

▶ Discuss, write or present.

1. We heard about the possible reasons why dancing lessons benefit people with Parkinson's, but what do you think is most important? Is it the physical aspect of dancing, or the mental aspect of learning, or just having fun with other people with the same problems?

2. The second man talked about the mental barrier, and said that in order to benefit from the lessons you had to be really up for it, and motivated. Do you agree with this? Can you think of any other situations in which it is important to be really motivated?

3. Do you enjoy watching professional dancing, such as ballet or stage musicals? Describe a performance that you have seen.

Unit 9

The Battersea Academy

イギリスのとある動物保護団体に世界中から関心が寄せられています。彼らの新しい活動について、ニュースを見てみましょう。

Starting Off

1 Setting the Scene

▶ **What do you think?**

1. Do you know anybody who owns a dog or a cat? Do they treat them well?
2. If you own a dog or cat in a city, how should you treat it? What are the most important things to do? Is there any difference between looking after cats and dogs?
3. Have you ever heard of a dog or cat being badly treated, or even thrown away? What happened?

2 Building Language

▶ **For each word (1-5), find two synonyms (a-j).**

1. abandon   [   ] [   ]
2. welfare   [   ] [   ]
3. expertise   [   ] [   ]
4. distress   [   ] [   ]
5. stray   [   ] [   ]

a. lost
b. prosperity
c. well-being
d. knowledge
e. runaway

f. trouble
g. leave behind
h. hardship
i. skill
j. discard

3 Understanding Check 1

▶ **Read the quotes, then watch the news and match them to the right people.**

1. We would like to know how we could improve our score on that one ...
    [   ]

2. ... their own academy, to train up teams and show them how they do it.
    [   ]

3. Now most of us are aware of the work that Battersea do with rehoming dogs ...
    [   ]

4. We take them through the entire rehoming journey, ...
    [   ]

4 Understanding Check 2

▶ **Which is the best answer?**

1. What is Battersea Dogs and Cats Home famous for around the world?
    a. It looks after abandoned animals, and finds new homes for them.
    b. It looks after people's pets when they go on holiday.
    c. People can stay there and play with the animals.
    d. It is a hospital for sick cats and dogs.

2. According to the video, which one of the following sentences is correct?
    a. The Home gets hundreds of requests to come and visit, and the delegates are there for five weeks.
    b. There are 70 million stray dogs in India, and the delegates get 70 distress calls a day.
    c. In India, there are 30 million stray dogs, and the delegates get 60 distress calls a week.
    d. The Home gets thousands of requests to come and visit, and the delegates are there for five days.

3. If you phone to book a course for the summer, what answer do you think you will get?
    a. "Yes, of course. How many people will be coming?"
    b. "We only have places for people from Spain, Cyprus or Mauritius."
    c. "I'm sorry. I'm afraid all the courses are already booked up."
    d. "Oh, I'm sorry. I'm afraid the courses have been cancelled because of illness."

▶ **What do you remember?**

4. Why has the Battersea Dogs and Cats Home launched an academy?

_____

5. What is the biggest challenge for the Indian delegates?

_____

6. What are the visitors particularly interested in?

_____

BACKGROUND INFORMATION

　今回のニュースに登場した「バタシー・ドッグズ・アンド・キャッツ・ホーム (the Battersea Dogs and Cats Home)」は、バタシーにあるロンドン・センター (the London Centre) の他に、バークシャー (Berkshire) のオールド・ウィンザー・センター (the Old Windsor Centre)、ケントのブランズ・ハッチ・センター (the Brands Hatch Centre) を運営する民間の動物保護団体です。メアリー・ティールビー (Mary Tealby, 1801-65) によって1860年に設立され、現在までに310万匹以上の犬や猫の世話をしています。2018年のデータによると、バタシーは年間7,000匹の犬や猫を引き取って世話をし、1,225匹に新しい飼い主を見つけました。

　しかし、健康状態の悪さや獰猛さによって、バタシーで殺処分される犬や猫もいます。2009年にバタシーが引き取った7,866匹のうち、3分の1にあたる1,931匹が、健康状態に問題がないにもかかわらず新しい引き取り手が見つからないほど凶暴だという理由で殺処分されました。とりわけ、獰猛なスタッフォードシャー・ブルテリア (Staffordshire Bull Terrier) はペットとして人気がある一方、飼い主の手に負えないとしてバタシーに引き取られることが多く、その数は1996年の396匹から2009年の3,600匹へと増加しました。ですが、近年、バタシーは犬の殺処分よりも再訓練に力を入れています。

　2020年3月以降の新型コロナウイルスの感染拡大は、バタシーの犬猫にまで思わぬ影響を与えました。都市封鎖で外出を禁止され、家に閉じ込められた人々がペットに癒しを求めた結果、バタシーの犬猫の引き取り希望が急増したのです。バタシーに保護されている犬猫の数は60匹程度に減少して、それぞれに十分なケアが行き届くようになり、図らずも彼らにとっては幸せな状況となりました。

参考：

https://www.battersea.org.uk
https://www.telegraph.co.uk/lifestyle/pets/7921277/Thousands-of-healthy-dogs-put-down-because-of-rise-in-dangerous-strays.html
https://www.standard.co.uk/news/uk/battersea-dogs-and-cats-home-pets-loving-life-lockdown-a4442466.html

5 Filling Gaps   News Story   ⊙ CD2-02 [Original] ⊙ CD2-03 [Voiced]

▶ **Watch the news, then fill the gaps in the text.**

Newsreader: Now Battersea Dogs and Cats Home is known around the world for the work it does caring and rehoming (**1**   ) and (**2**   ) animals, and it seems international (**3**   ) groups are keen to learn from them. So they've (**4**   ) their own academy, to train up teams and show them how they do it. Sonja Jessup has more.

First woman: This is Binky. She is a three-year-old greyhound.

Sonja Jessup: (**5**   ) out the way, Binky can get on with helping with the lessons here at the new Battersea Academy, and listening in, visitors from animal (**6**   ) teams across India. They've (**7**   ) to London for one of the first courses of its kind.

Jessup: Now most of us are aware of the work that Battersea do with rehoming dogs like Gizmo here. But the academy is about sharing some of their (**8**   ) with groups from around the world. They say they get thousands of (**9**   ) to come and visit, and this is a way of (**10**   ) them in, and showing them what they really do.

Paul Marvell, Executive Head, Battersea Academy: Our delegates are with us for five days. We take them through the entire rehoming journey, from the moment a dog or cat (**11**   ) Battersea, through to the moment it (**12**   ) us and goes to its forever home.

Jessup: And these are just some of the challenges (**13**   ) those visitors back home. It's thought there are around 30 million (**14**   ) dogs on the streets of India.

Geeta Seshamani, Vice President, Friendicoes: It's not unusual to get 60 to 70 (**15**   ) calls a day for animals that need to be picked up because they're sick or (**16**   ) or hit and run. Um, it's also the public brings in animals and (**17**   ) them at the gate. So I think our biggest challenge is (**18**   ) (**19**   ) the large number of animals that are given to us.

Second woman: He doesn't like the thing round his neck he says.

5

10

15

20

25

30

35

52

Third woman: Oh, I know. I don't like it either.

Jessup: And it's what happens to the dogs once they're ready to leave Battersea, that visitors are (^{20}) interested in.

40

Seshamani: They also seem to have an (^{21}) record for rehoming. We would like to know how we could improve our score on that one, because it's so (^{22}) to take an animal that is almost half dead off the streets, care for it and then get it a good home.

45

First woman: Good girl. Well done.

Jessup: Battersea says its courses are already (^{23}) (^{24}) over the summer, with future students from Spain, Cyprus and Mauritius. And Binky here? She's proving to be quite the teacher's pet. Sonja Jessup, BBC London News.   *(Friday 19 April 2019)*

50

Notes

l.1 **Battersea Dogs and Cats Home**「バタシー・ドッグズ・アンド・キャッツ・ホーム」犬や猫の保護活動を行っている団体。ロンドンのバタシーなど3か所に拠点を持つ。1860年設立　l.9 **greyhound**「グレイハウンド」ヨーロッパ原産の狩猟犬種　l.26 **Friendicoes**「フレンディコズ」インドのデリーにある病院つきの動物保護施設。1979年設立

動物の児童文学

　子供の想像力においては、動物が人間のように話したり振る舞ったりするのは自然なことであり、動物を描いた児童文学は枚挙にいとまがありません。ファンタジー大国イギリスで、動物の登場する児童文学の代表的なものには、ビアトリクス・ポター (Beatrix Potter, 1866-1943) の『ピーター・ラビットのおはなし』(*The Tale of Peter Rabbit*, 1902) シリーズ、ケネス・グレアム (Kenneth Grahame, 1859-1932) の『たのしい川べ』(*The Wind in the Willows*, 1908)、ヒュー・ロフティング (Hugh Lofting, 1886-1947) のドリトル先生 (Dr. Dolittle) シリーズ、A. A. ミルン (A. A. Milne, 1882-1956) の『クマのプーさん』(*Winnie-the-Pooh*, 1926) シリーズ、ルイス・キャロル (Lewis Carroll, 1832-98) の『不思議の国のアリス』(*Alice in Wonderland*, 1865)、C. S. ルイス (C. S. Lewis, 1898-1963) の『ナルニア国物語』(*The Chronicles of Narnia*, 1950-56) などがあります。国民の４人に１人がペットを飼うと言われる動物愛護の精神は、こうして養われるのでしょうか。

Moving On

6 Making a Summary

CD2-04

▶ Fill the gaps to complete the summary.

　Battersea Dogs and Cats Home cares for, and rehomes (s　　　　　) and (a　　　　　) animals. They have recently (l　　　　　) an academy so that they can invite (w　　　　　) groups from all around the world. They have thousands of requests to come to their courses, and this is a way in which they can share their (e　　　　　). Members of Indian animal rescue teams were among the first to visit, and will be there for five days. Their biggest challenge in India is dealing with the large number of animals. They often get 60 to 70 (d　　　　　) calls a day, about sick or (a　　　　　) animals, and also the public just (d　　　　　) animals at their gate. They are particularly interested in learning how to rehome animals, as Battersea has an excellent (r　　　　　) in doing this. Its summer courses are already fully booked, with future students coming from Spain, Cyprus and Mauritius.

7 Follow Up

▶ Discuss, write or present.

1. What do you think of the work that Battersea Dogs and Cats Home is doing? Do you think it is important work? Why do people abandon animals?

2. Is there a similar place or organisation in Japan that helps unwanted animals? Is it well-known or successful?

3. The Battersea Dogs and Cats Home tries very hard to rehome abandoned dogs and cats. Would you be interested in adopting an animal from them and looking after it?

Students in Poverty

秋のイギリスで、新入生たちが大学生活の始まりに胸を躍らせています。ですが、深刻な面持ちの学生も少なくありません。彼らの新生活に影を落とす切実な問題について、ニュースを見てみましょう。

▌ Starting Off

1 Setting the Scene

▶ **What do you think?**

1. How much money do you think a student in Japan needs? What must they spend it on?

2. What can Japanese students do if they don't have enough money? Can they find help?

3. Do you know of anybody (not only students) who didn't have enough money for what they needed? What did they do about it? Did anybody help them?

2 Building Language

▶ **Which word (1-5) best fits which explanation (a-e)?**

1. deprived [ ]   a. estimate, based on available evidence
2. adapt [ ]   b. mark of disgrace that might harm your reputation
3. handful [ ]   c. poor; lacking adequate resources
4. assess [ ]   d. small amount or number
5. stigma [ ]   e. adjust or modify when conditions change

3 Understanding Check 1

▶ Read the quotes, then watch the news and match them to the right people.

1. … citing money problems as the reason why. [　]

2. … you wouldn't want to use it unless you have to. [　]

3. It's not an option. I'm not going to drop out. [　]

4. … so yes, I've got to save up and everything. [　]

4 Understanding Check 2

▶ Which is the best answer?

1. Why do students in Stoke need an average of £17,500 per year?
    a. This only pays for lectures.
    b. It's enough to pay for accommodation and living costs, but lectures are free.
    c. This pays for tuition fees, accommodation and living costs.
    d. It's enough for tuition, but accommodation is more expensive.

2. Approximately how many students gave up in the first year because of money problems?
    a. about 38% of them
    b. about 4% of them
    c. about 25% of them
    d. twenty-five students

3. Why must Ben pay more for his accommodation?
    a. His room at the YMCA was cheap, but now somebody else needs that room.
    b. The price of student accommodation has increased.
    c. He is now an adult, so he has to pay adult rent.
    d. Because he must study, he needs a much better room.

4. In what way is Staffordshire University different from most other universities?

_____

5. In what way is Ben not a typical student?

_____

6. Poor students can get free food at the food bank, so why is it never abused?

_____

BACKGROUND INFORMATION

　今回のニュースは、ストーク・オン・トレントにあるスタッフォードシャー大学のキャンパス内に「フードバンク(food banks)」が設置されたという話題です。フードバンクとは、品質に問題がないにもかかわらず市場で流通できなくなった食品を企業などから譲り受けて、生活困窮者に配給する活動および活動団体を指します。

　その始まりは、1967年に、アメリカ、アリゾナ州のフェニックスでジョン・ヴァン・ヘンゲル(John van Hengel)が、子供たちのためにスーパーマーケットのゴミ箱をあさる貧しい母親に出会ったことにあります。彼女は、要らなくなった食べ物が捨てられるのではなく、必要とする人々が持ち帰れるように、食べ物を蓄える「銀行」のような場所があればよいと提案しました。そこで、ヴァン・ヘンゲルは「セント・メリーズ・フードバンク(St. Mary's Food Bank)」という最初のフードバンクを開設しました。

　その後、フードバンクの活動は世界中に広まります。イギリスでは、2000年にパディー・ヘンダーソン(Paddy Henderson)が、自宅の物置きとガレージで「ソールズベリー・フードバンク(Salisbury Foodbank)」を始め、3日分の緊急の食べ物を地域の困窮した人々に与えたのが最初でした。

　さらに、ニュースにあるように、フードバンクの試みはイギリスの各地の大学に広がりました。その背景には、学生の貧困という社会問題があります。2015年の若者の貧困に関する調査によると、イギリスでは44万人の学生が貧困生活を送り、貧困状態の若者の25%を占めています。また、48%の学生が、貧困が学業に影響を与え、63%の学生が、貧困が食生活に影響を与えていると言います。この数字は新型コロナウイルス感染拡大による世界経済の停滞で、今後より一層増加することが予測されます。在学中は高騰する学費や住宅費の支払いに苦しみ、卒業後も学生ローンの返済が重くのしかかるというように、イギリスの学生の多くは貧困に喘いでいるのです。

参考：

https://www.feedingamerica.org/
https://www.trusselltrust.org/
https://www.independent.co.uk/student/news/university-of-east-anglia-launches-food-bank-initiative-to-help-tackle-rising-student-poverty-in-the-a6745701.html

5 Filling Gaps 　　 News Story 　　 ⊙ CD2-05 [Original] ⊙ CD2-06 [Voiced]

▶ **Watch the news, then fill the gaps in the text.**

Newsreader: Now, as new arrivals at universities across the country (¹ 　　　　) in to student life, the BBC has learnt that some universities have opened food banks on campuses, for students living in (² 　　　). Staffordshire University is one of them. More than a quarter of students there are from (³ 　　　) areas. Well, as part of a week of reports from Stoke-on-Trent, digital journalist Ben Moore and reporter Lucas Yeomans have been to see how the university is (⁴ 　　　) to the needs of students.

Lucas Yeomans: Welcome to the first week of the rest of your life. Yet (⁵ 　　　) all the clubs to join, societies to sign up for, and all the new friends to be made at Freshers' Week, students are only thinking about one thing.

First student: I think every student's got money and (⁶ 　　　) on the mind.

Second student: Money's going to really always be a problem 'cos I get like the lowest amount of maintenance loan.

Third student: I mean, it's been difficult ... so yes, I've got to save up and everything.

Yeomans: With (⁷ 　　　) (⁸ 　　　), accommodation and living costs, students in Stoke need to find an average of about seventeen and a half thousand pounds a year before they can even start lectures.

Ben Moore: I left school with, um, no qualifications, eh, ended up getting kicked out, and then, after that, er, I got made (⁹ 　　　).

Yeomans: Ben is not your (¹⁰ 　　　) student.

Moore: I know it's going to be a (¹¹ 　　　). I know with student loans and stuff. I know I'm just going to have to, what spare time I have got, I'm going to have to work and stuff, and just get that (¹² 　　　) money.

Yeomans: Stoke takes more than a quarter of its students from (¹³ 　　　) areas, many from the local area, which creates a (¹⁴ 　　　) set of problems.

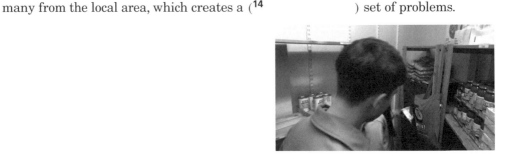

Yeomans: According to the latest figures from Staffordshire University, 38 first-year students dropped out (^{15}) in the 2016 to 2017 academic year, 30 citing money problems as the reason why. What that basically means is, one in 25 students had to stop studying because they couldn't (^{16}) to.

Yeomans: That may be why Staffordshire is one of only a (^{17}) of campuses with a food bank on site.

Geeta Lal, member of staff of Student Union: Yeah, so we've got everything. We've 35 got all the pasta and stuff here, the dried ingredients and ...

Lal: It comes through an adviser, either through the university or ourselves. Um, they (^{18}) what the best route is to help our student, so it's never abused, um, and, because of the (^{19}) of using food banks anyway, you wouldn't want to use it unless you have to. 40

Yeomans: Ben is about to move into a student accommodation. He's been at Stoke's YMCA for 5 years since he came off the streets, but now he's at university, someone else needs his room.

Moore: My standard (^{20}) is £15 a week to, to live here. Um, the house that I'm going to be staying in, costs £75 a week to live in. I don't ... I haven't really 45 been thinking about it as of yet.

Yeomans: It's a hard three years ahead, but Ben won't let his past (^{21}) his future.

Moore: This is kind of, (^{22}) (^{23}) (^{24}) for me. And that's, that's how I look at it. It's not an option. I'm not going to drop out. 50 That's it.

Yeomans: Lucas Yeomans, BBC News, Stoke.

(Friday 27 September 2019)

BEHIND THE SCENES

イギリスのチャリティー

　チャリティーは、イギリス人の生活にしっかりと根付いている行為です。街を歩けば「オックスファム (Oxfam)」などのチャリティー・ショップが点在し、中古品の売買が抵抗なく行われています。マラソンなどのスポーツイベントでは、真剣に記録を狙うランナーに混じり、仮装して注目を集めようとするチャリティー・ランナーもいます。人の集まるパーティーやコンサートなどで「チャリティー・ラッフル (charity raffle)」という賞品の当たるクジが販売され、「オープン・ガーデン (open garden)」という個人宅の庭園を解放する行事もチャリティーです。ホームレスに販売を任せる雑誌『ビッグ・イシュー』(Big Issue) もイギリス発祥ですし、1988年に「コミック・リリーフ (Comic Relief)」という慈善団体が始めた「レッド・ノーズ・デー (Red Nose Day)」は、今ではアメリカにも広がっています。

Moving On

6 Making a Summary

 CD2-07

▶ Fill the gaps to complete the summary.

　A lot of university students in Britain are living in (p⎽⎽⎽⎽⎽⎽⎽). They need about £17,500 a year for tuition, accommodation and living costs, and for some people, this is difficult to find. More than a quarter of Staffordshire University students come from (d⎽⎽⎽⎽⎽⎽⎽) areas, and 4% drop out in the first year due to money problems. That is why it is one of a (h⎽⎽⎽⎽⎽⎽⎽) of universities to (a⎽⎽⎽⎽⎽⎽⎽) to the needs of the students and open a food bank. Their advisers (a⎽⎽⎽⎽⎽⎽⎽) the best way to help the students, and although the food is free, the food banks are not abused, because of the (s⎽⎽⎽⎽⎽⎽⎽) of appearing to be poor. Ben Moore is one student for whom life is going to be a (s⎽⎽⎽⎽⎽⎽⎽). He left school with no qualifications, but now dropping out is not an (o⎽⎽⎽⎽⎽⎽⎽). He now has to pay £75 a week for student accommodation, and will get a job to find the money if he has to.

7 Follow Up

▶ Discuss, write or present.

1. You discussed Japanese students in Part One. Compare the Japanese situation with the British situation. Do you think Ben could afford to attend a Japanese university?

2. There are many similar food banks in Britain. Do you think they are a good idea? Is there also a stigma about using such food banks in Japan?

3. What do you think of Ben? He was kicked out of school with no qualifications, and was homeless for a while. Yet he has got into university and is determined to succeed. Do you know anybody else like that? Would it be possible in Japan?

The Importance of Creative Subjects

近年、イギリスで美術の授業が減少しつつあります。それによりどのような問題が生じるのでしょうか。ニュースを見てみましょう。

▌▌ Starting Off

1 Setting the Scene

▶ **What do you think?**

1. What subjects did you study (or are you studying) at school? Which of these subjects do you think are 'creative' subjects?

2. Which subjects do you think are the most important? Write a list, from the most important to the least important.

3. Why do you think people study art?

2 Building Language

▶ **Which word or phrase (1-5) best fits which explanation (a-e)?**

1. grass roots   [   ]   **a.** cover with something soft, like paint, mud or plaster

2. doodle   [   ]   **b.** scribble or draw aimlessly, without purpose

3. daub   [   ]   **c.** add to something, make it complete

4. complement   [   ]   **d.** harmful, causing damage

5. detrimental   [   ]   **e.** the origin, basis, or beginnings of something

3 Understanding Check 1

▶ Read the quotes, then watch the news and match them to the right people.

1. ... they'd be kind enough to spend their own money and bring stuff in. [   ]

2. UK industries also want more art on the curriculum. [   ]

3. It comes up in English, it comes up in maths ... [   ]

4. People don't study art just to become artists or art historians. [   ]

4 Understanding Check 2

▶ Which is the best answer?

1. According to the video, which of the following is correct?
   a. Because creative industries are no longer so important in the UK, the number of students studying art and design has fallen by 2%.
   b. Because so many students are choosing to study art, creative industries have become very important for the UK economy.
   c. Although the creative industries are very important for the UK economy, the number of students taking art and design at A-level has decreased by 7%.
   d. Last year, an estimated hundred billion pounds was invested in art education.

2. Why don't art departments have enough money? Which of the following was <u>not</u> suggested as a reason?
   a. Most of the money goes to the STEM subjects, and not the art subjects.
   b. Inflation has increased faster than funding.
   c. There are more pupils at schools.
   d. The number of pupils studying art has decreased.

3. According to UK industry, what should young people do to make it easier to get a job?
   a. They should study both a science subject and an art subject.
   b. They should concentrate on the STEM subjects to get technical skills.
   c. They should try to increase their creativity, and not worry about sciences.
   d. They should study marketing, with creativity and technical skills.

‣ **What do you remember?**

4. According to opinions in the video, why is the decrease in students taking art subjects a bad thing?

_____

5. According to the female art teacher, why do people study art?

_____

6. According to the man in the balcony, why is an art education important?

_____

BACKGROUND INFORMATION

　イギリスの演劇や音楽といった芸術活動は、世界でも有数の高い水準を保っており、芸術産業は重要な地位を占めています。しかし近年芸術科目は、学校の正規のカリキュラムから削られたり、専任の先生が雇用されないなど、生徒が履修する機会は減りつつあります。

　このような変化の一因となったのが、2010年から行われた学校の評価基準の改革です。以前は数学と英語を含む全科目でA*からC評価を取った生徒の割合から計算されていましたが、この改革により16歳で受けるGCSEの結果を学校ごとにまとめた統計を出す際に、EBacc (English Baccalaureate) とProgress 8と呼ばれる2つの基準が設けられました。EBaccというのは、大学で学び専門職につくために必須の科目群で、英語・英文学、STEM(science, technology, engineering, mathematics) と総称される科学の教科、言語からなり、政府は2022年までに75%、2025年までに90%の生徒がこれらの科目でGCSEを受験することを目標に掲げています。Progress 8は、4つのカテゴリーに分けられた最高8科目の点数から算出され、全国の中学校の中での位置を可視化します。最重要科目である英語と数学は、その重要度からそれぞれ2倍で計算され、3つ目のカテゴリーは、科学、コンピューター科学、歴史、地理、言語から3教科、そして最後のカテゴリーは芸術を含むそれ以外の科目から3教科です。Progress 8で学校の判定を出す際には、EBaccに含まれる諸科目が重視されます。

　2012年には、GCSEそのものを廃止してEBaccにより重点を置いたEBC (English Baccalaureate Certificate) という新しい試験を導入する計画がありましたが、頓挫しました。試験制度そのものは維持されましたが、生徒や親の学校選びに直結する学校評価で芸術科目が軽視されることになり、学校でも限られた予算を重要科目に当てざるを得ない背景があります。しかし、芸術家が声明を出したり、生徒の要望もあり、学校は板挟みになっています。

参考：
https://www.bbc.com/news/education-21365373
https://www.bbc.com/news/education-42862996
https://culturallearningalliance.org.uk/what-is-the-current-state-of-the-arts-in-schools/
https://www.bbc.com/news/uk-45171371

5 Filling Gaps | News Story

CD2-08 [Original] · CD2-09 [Voiced]

▶ Watch the news, then fill the gaps in the text.

Newsreader: The creative industries is worth an estimated a hundred billion pounds to the UK economy. Yet, the number of pupils taking art subjects at school has been (**1**   ) for the last five years, with teachers saying (**2**   ) in this sector is being cut off at the (**3**   ) (**4**   ). A director of a leading arts institution believes it's even having a (**5**   ) effect on young people's ability to understand the world around them. Here's Wendy Hurrell with the first of her reports, looking at arts education.

5

10

Wendy Hurrell: Most of us have a (**6**   ), paint (**7**   ) masterpiece hidden away somewhere from when we were very young. Some turn it into a (**8**   ).

Estelle Lovatt, art lecturer: I like the way as well that some of the foliage comes out.   15

Hurrell: These students at the Insight School of Art in Whetstone are learning the business side of the art world, along with their studio (**9**   ) sessions.

Lovatt: Oh, yeah, wow.

Hurrell: And there's a growing awareness that studying art can (**10**   ) other careers, too.   20

Lovatt: People don't study art just to become artists or art historians. People study art to become vets, policemen, accountants, chefs. If we close the art door to these young people, and don't allow them to study, and to become artists or art historians or anything else that they want to be, it will be (**11**   ) to our place in the civilised world. It's that serious.   25

Hurrell: In fact there has been a slight increase in the number of students taking Art and Design GCSE, up 2% in the last five years. But in the same period it fell by 7% at A-level.

Lovatt: I like the way that, that you've also made her quite glamorous with the earing there ...

30

64

Hurrell: These students have paid for this summer course, finding that schools can't always (¹²   ) resources. There are (¹³   ) in budgets because school (¹⁴   ) hasn't kept up with inflation, and there are more pupils.

Leondres Benissan, art student: It's as if we've been put as a second thought really, because most of the (¹⁵   ) goes to the more important subjects, as they'd call it. It's as little as pencils in the art department. There wouldn't be enough and some teachers, they'd be kind enough to spend their own money and bring stuff in.

Hurrell: With social media and computer communication, we live in an (¹⁶   ) image-based world.

Stefan Kalmár, Institute of Contemporary Arts: If you look, er, how politics is (¹⁷   ). If you look at the American elections, at Brexit, er, the visual, er, plays a huge role, er, in the current economy of 21st century politics. Like writing, and reading it has to start fro-, from a young age because only if you understand how an image is made and that you can then make your own image, you can understand world.

Hurrell: UK industries also want more art on the curriculum. They say adding it to the STEM subjects — science, technology, engineering and maths — would give young people a (¹⁸   ) combination of creativity and technical skill.

Student: It should be used in more lessons other than if you choose it. It allows you to develop your ideas. It comes up in English, it comes up in maths with analysing 3-D shapes or analysing a story and coming up with something completely fresh and creative off the top of your head. It's just a very important subject.

Lovatt: Yeah, yeah, yeah.

Hurrell: And these young people say there's almost a (¹⁹   ) attached to studying the so-called soft subjects. Extra government (²⁰   ) announced this week may go some way to placing greater emphasis on the arts, maintaining London as a world leader. Wendy Hurrell, BBC London.

(Tuesday 3 September 2019)

Notes

l.16 **the Insight School of Art**「インサイト美術学校」ウェットストーンにある美術学校。成人クラス、児童クラス、アーティストを目指すクラスがある。2001年創設　l.27 **GCSE**「一般中等教育修了試験」イギリスで義務教育修了時である16歳で受ける試験　l.28 **A-level**「一般教育修了上級レベル」イギリスで中等教育卒業もしくは大学入学レベルにあることを示す学業修了認定　l.41 **Institute of Contemporary Arts**「現代美術協会」王立芸術院のような伝統的な芸術観に対抗するためロンドンに設立された芸術文化センター。1947年創設　l.42 **Brexit**「イギリスのEU（欧州連合）離脱」　l.47 **the STEM subjects**「基幹科目」Science, Technology, Engineering, Mathsの頭文字を取って主要科目をこう呼ぶ。〈p.63参照〉　l.56 **soft subjects**「主要でない科目」他に心理学、演劇、メディアなどがある。反意語はhard subjectで、数学、歴史、化学、英文学、経済学などが含まれる

路面アートの世界

　子供がチョークで道路に落書きをして遊ぶことがありますが、実は、歴史ある芸術の一種です。路面アーティスト (pavement artist) の起源は、16世紀イタリアにおいて「聖母画家 (madonnaro)」と呼ばれた旅の芸術家たちでした。彼らは各地を渡り歩いて聖母像 (Madonna) などの宗教画を路面に描き、道行く人々から投げ銭を貰って生活していました。また、19世紀のロンドンにも、「大道絵師 (screever)」と呼ばれる路面アーティストが数多く存在しました。イタリア語で「書く」を意味する scrivere に由来しており、宗教や政治にまつわる絵を描き、詩や教訓などの言葉を書き添えたことからその名がついたとされています。こうした歴史のある路面アートは、現代では3Dの技法を取り入れるなどして進化を遂げ、子供から大人まで、誰もが体験して楽しめる、より身近な芸術として親しまれています。

Moving On

6 Making a Summary

▶ **Fill the gaps to complete the summary.**

　Many of us have a (d　　　　　　　), paint (d　　　　　　　) masterpiece hidden away. Studying art can help people understand the world, and if people stopped studying art, it would be (d　　　　　　) to our place in the civilised world. One view is that art can (c　　　　　　) other careers, and should be studied together with the (S　　　　　　) subjects. However, although the creative industries are very important for the UK economy, the number of pupils studying art at A-level has fallen, and investment is being cut off at the (g　　　　　　) (r　　　　　　). (F　　　　　　) has decreased because of inflation, increased numbers of pupils, and demands of more important subjects. Young people also say there is a (s　　　　　　) attached to studying the so-called (s　　　　　　) subjects. Luckily, however, extra government (f　　　　　　) has been announced.

7 Follow Up

▶ **Discuss, write or present.**

1. Do you agree that studying art helps us to understand the world around us? If we don't allow people to study art, would it be "detrimental to our place in the civilised world"?

2. Think about your own studies of art. Did they help you to develop ideas in other subjects? For example, did they help you to "come up with something completely fresh and creative", as the student said?

3. Is the situation the same in Japan? Are fewer people studying art? Does the government think 'STEM' subjects are more important?

Unit 12

New Rules for Drones

愛好家が競って求めるドローンですが、性能が高まるあまり、野放しにはできなくなってきました。規制などの対策が取られるようになってきましたが、イギリスの現状はどうなのでしょうか。ニュースを見てみましょう。

Starting Off

1 Setting the Scene

▶ What do you think?

1. Why do you think people own and use drones?
2. What problems do drones cause, and why do some people dislike them?
3. Have you ever been stuck at an airport or station? What was the reason? How did you feel?

2 Building Language

Which word or phrase (1-5) best fits which explanation (a-e)?

1. standstill   [   ]   a. be in agreement with, or act on, a decision or rule
2. restriction   [   ]   b. something that confines you or keeps you within limits
3. fall foul   [   ]   c. very much, a lot
4. appreciably   [   ]   d. get into trouble by not following a rule or regulation
5. abide by   [   ]   e. a complete stop, with no movement at all

Watching the News

3 Understanding Check 1

▶ **Read the quotes, then watch the news and match them to the right people.**

1. Before this weekend, any one of us could buy almost any type of drone ... [   ]

2. Well, to stop the same thing happening again ... [   ]

3. ... so that we encourage more people to use it. [   ]

4. Just get a feel for what the controls do. [   ]

4 Understanding Check 2

▶ **Which is the best answer?**

1. Which sentence is correct, according to the video?
   a. Hundreds of thousands of people are going to register their drones tonight.
   b. Tonight is the deadline for drone pilots to register their drones, but so far fewer than half have done so.
   c. More than half of the country's drone pilots brought Gatwick Airport to a standstill.
   d. Gatwick Airport was brought to a standstill by hundreds of thousands of people.

2. In order to register a drone now what must a pilot do?
   a. A pilot must pay a thousand pounds.
   b. A pilot must fly their drones at maximum height.
   c. A pilot must pass a special test about flying drones.
   d. A pilot must talk with a drone pilot instructor.

3. According to Burridge, why will it not be easy to police the new rules?
   a. There are too many drones.
   b. It is not yet possible to identify a drone and link it to its owner.
   c. The police do not yet know how to fly drones.
   d. There is no system in place for following drones.

▶ What do you remember?

4. Before that weekend what were the only rules for flying drones in an open field?

_____

5. Why doesn't the drone pilot instructor think the new rules will make much difference?

_____

6. What is the cost of registration, and why is it so reasonable?

_____

BACKGROUND INFORMATION

　2018年12月19日、ロンドン近郊のガトウィック空港（Gatwick Airport）が突如閉鎖となりました。事の発端は、2機のドローンが滑走路の上空を飛んでいるという情報が寄せられたことでした。翌20日にもドローンの目撃情報が相次ぎ、21日にはようやく安全が確認されましたが、10万人以上の乗客と1,000便近くのフライトに多大な影響が生じました。警察と軍が出動して捜査にあたったところ、近郊に住む2人の容疑者が逮捕されましたが、証拠不十分で罪には問われませんでした。目撃情報自体の信憑性を疑う声もあり、なおも事件は未解決のままですが、結果としてドローンの使用法や規制を検討する大きな契機となりました。

　ニュースで取り上げられていた今回の規制以降、一定の基準を超える重量のドローンを所有するには、操縦士としてのID登録をし、IDを示すラベルを機体に貼らなければならなくなりました。また、所有せずとも、一定の大きさ以上のドローンを飛行させる場合には、オンラインのテストを受験して許可証を取得する必要があります。テストは20問の選択問題となっており、16問以上正解すれば合格となります。実際にドローンを飛行させる際にも様々な規則があり、例えば、航空機や空港、飛行場からは十分な距離を取る必要があるのはもちろん、人、建物、車、電車、船の50メートル以内を飛行させてはいけません。さらに、人や建物が密集した場所では150メートル以内に機体を近づけてはいけないなど、安全を保つための項目が設けられています。

　こうして規制が進むかのように思われましたが、2019年の年末時点で、イギリス国内に13万人いると思われるドローンユーザーのうち、登録を済ませたのは約8万人でした。また、2020年のコロナウイルスによる都市封鎖期間中はドローンの不正な使用が相次ぎ、頭上のすぐ近くを飛ぶドローンやプライバシーの侵害への苦情が警察に多数寄せられました。問題の解消にはなおも時間がかかりそうです。

参考：
https://www.bbc.com/news/uk-england-sussex-46623754
https://www.caa.co.uk/Consumers/Unmanned-aircraft/Our-role/Drone-and-model-aircraft-registration/
https://www.independent.co.uk/news/uk/crime/coronavirus-lockdown-uk-drones-illegal-use-police-wiltshire-west-mercia-a9507376.html

5 Filling Gaps | News Story

▶ Watch the news, then fill the gaps in the text.

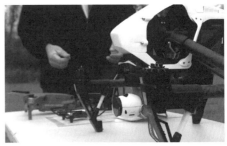

Newsreader: Now in the run up to last Christmas, Gatwick Airport was brought to a (¹   ) by drones. Well, to stop the same thing happening again, hundreds of thousands of people have until tonight to register their drones. But with (²   ) running out, the Civil Aviation Authority says not even half the country's drone pilots have done so. Here's our transport correspondent, Tom Burridge.

Tom Burridge: Before this weekend, any one of us could buy almost any type of drone online or from a shop, and fly it safely in an open field away from people, buildings and (³   ). As long as you don't lose sight of it, fly it in an airport's exclusion zone, or above 400 feet. But now there are new (⁴   ). (⁵   ) (⁶   ) of the new rules, and you could face a one thousand pound (⁷   ).

Simon Smith, a pilot instructor, Phantom Flight School: At just 80 grams, this is well under 250, so it isn't (⁸   ) by the new regulations.

Burridge: OK.

Smith: Whereas these two drones are (⁹   ) heavier than 250 grams ...

Burridge: So the new rules apply.

Smith: And the new rules therefore apply.

Smith: Let's just take it up to (¹⁰   ) height.

Burridge: Talking us through the new rules is drone pilot (¹¹   ) Simon Smith.

Smith: Support mode.

Burridge: The first big change is that, before a beginner like me can take the controls ...

Smith: Right and left.

Burridge: ... it's off to the classroom.

Burridge: And when must you have (¹²   ) for flying your drone or model aircraft?

Burridge: A twenty-question, multiple-choice (¹³   ).

Burridge: Which of these is the main reason for not flying above 400 feet?

Burridge: Anyone of any age can still fly a standard-sized drone. But you have to pass this test first.

Burridge: Yay. I passed.

Burridge: I just press up.

Burridge: So now, I'm allowed to fly a drone …

Smith: There we go.

Burridge: … for the first time.

Smith: Just get a feel for what the controls do.

Burridge: But this is only OK because the drone belongs to Simon, and he's registered.

Burridge: The person (^{14}) for a drone like this one has to register it now. They have to be over 18. The cost of doing so is a (^{15}) nine pounds.

Burridge: For Simon, it's a step in the right direction but …

Smith: Do I think it'll make much difference? Honestly, no. The people that, er, (^{16}) (^{17}) the rules and regulations, um, will (^{18}) (^{19}) them whether they are registered or not.

Burridge: Tens of thousands of drone users still haven't registered. And that empty runway at Gatwick, and the misery passengers felt for days when drones were apparently (^{20}) last December means airports hope more people will sign up via the Civil Aviation Authority's new system.

Karen Dee, Airport Operators Association: It is a concern to us that we haven't, you know, got everybody on board yet. And we want to, er, encourage the CAA and government to ensure that they (^{21}) this, that they keep the costs to those individuals at a reasonable level so that we encourage more people to use it.

Burridge: Simple technology could (^{22}) identify a drone, and link it to its owner. But such a system is still not in place, so the new rules won't be easy to police. Tom Burridge, BBC News in Kent. *(Friday 29 November 2019)*

Notes

l.2 **Gatwick Airport**「ガトウィック空港」ロンドンの南サリー州にある国際空港　l.7 **the Civil Aviation Authority** (CAA)「民間航空局」航空会社・空港の活動を監視・規制する独立機関　l.16 **Phantom Flight School**「ファントム飛行学校」ドローンの操縦を指導する教習所　l.56 **Airport Operators Association**「空港運営者協会」英国の空港の利益を代表する業界団体であり、空港の問題について英国政府および規制当局と関与する主要機関　l.63 **Kent**「ケント」イングランド南東部の州

Moving On

6 Making a Summary

 CD2-13

▶ **Fill the gaps to complete the summary.**

　Just before Christmas 2018, Gatwick Airport was brought to a (s　　　　　　) by drones that were (s　　　　　) nearby. Because of this, the Civil Aviation Authority have introduced a new system of drone (r　　　　　). Before that weekend, almost anybody could fly a drone as long as they didn't lose sight of it, fly it over 400 feet, or near an airport. Now, however, some (r　　　　　) have been introduced, and if you (f　　　　　) (f　　　　　) of these new rules, you could face a one thousand pound fine. The rules only apply to drones over 250 grams but two drones in the video were (a　　　　　) heavier than that. The most important (r　　　　　) is that all drone pilots must take a test. However, Simon Smith, a drone instructor, thinks people who (a　　　　　) by the rules will (a　　　　　) by them whether they are registered or not. (R　　　　　) only costs nine pounds, but so far fewer than half of drone pilots had applied.

7 Follow Up

▶ **Discuss, write or present.**

1. What do you think of this registration scheme? Do you think that taking the 20 question test will make the drone pilots better, and abide by the rules?

2. Why do you think drones were flying around Gatwick Airport? Do you think that this was a serious crime? Did the airport do the right thing by delaying flights?

3. Are there many drones in Japan? Do they cause any problems? Is there a similar system of registration?

Unit **13**

Pride in London

ロンドンでイギリス史上最大のプライド・パレードが行われました。どのような人々が参加したのでしょうか。ニュースを見てみましょう。

Starting Off

1 Setting the Scene

▶ **What do you think?**

1. Do you enjoy street parades and festivals? What is your favourite one?
2. Why do people organise parades? What are some of the reasons?
3. Why do you think LGBT people organise big parades every year?

2 Building Language

▶ **For each word (1-5), find two synonyms (a-j).**

1. confrontation   [   ] [   ]
2. diversity   [   ] [   ]
3. solidarity   [   ] [   ]
4. flagship   [   ] [   ]
5. polarise   [   ] [   ]

a. separate
b. support
c. divide
d. dispute
e. variety
f. leading
g. main
h. unity
i. fight
j. difference

3 Understanding Check 1

▶ **Read the quotes, then watch the news and match them to the right people.**

1. ... with many of them marching for the very first time.   [   ]

2. ... our history, our her-story and our their-story.   [   ]

3. ... an all-singing, all-dancing carnival of colour.   [   ]

4. We have a place here. Everyone is equal.   [   ]

4 Understanding Check 2

▶ **Which is the best answer?**

1. What was that year's Pride march celebrating?
   a. the end of violent confrontations between police and gay activists in London
   b. the 50th anniversary of homosexuality being made legal in the UK
   c. the 50th anniversary of the first Stonewall uprising in New York
   d. the introduction of same-sex marriage

2. What was the central theme of the march?
   a. solidarity
   b. peace
   c. equality
   d. diversity

3. Which of the following is correct?
   a. More than 1.5 million marched in the parade while 30,000 people watched it.
   b. About 600 organisations and corporations were marching for the first time.
   c. 30,000 people marched in the parade while more than 1.5 million watched it.
   d. 30,000 people in the parade were being watched by 600 organisations and corporations.

▶ **What do you remember?**

4. The first man said that no matter what race, religion or sexuality they belong to, they are something. What did he say they were?

_____

5. Why had some activists called for the Pride event to return to its roots as a protest?

_____

6. According to Hunte, why were the people at the parade happy?

_____

BACKGROUND INFORMATION

　2019年のロンドン・プライド・パレードは、1か月に渡る様々な行事の締めくくりとして、7月6日の土曜日に盛大に開催されました。一連の行事は6月8日に始まり、演劇、ダンス、アート、映画、パーティーなど90以上の催しを通して、LGBT文化に焦点が当てられました。ロンドンのプライド・パレードは、「ストーンウォールの反乱」(p. 77参照)の3周年に当たる1972年以来毎年開催されています。パレードは、正午にロンドン市長サディク・カーン (Sadiq Khan, 1970-) の開会の辞で始まり、リージェント・ストリートを出発し、オックスフォード・サーカス、ピカデリー・サーカス経由でゴールのトラファルガー広場へと進みました。ロンドンの中心部を、多彩な衣服に身を包んだ参加者が練り歩きました。

　参加者が増え、規模が大きくなったパレードに対して、商業主義の台頭を非難する声も聞かれましたが、主催者側は、大規模イベントの1つの側面として肯定的に捉えており、また政治的メッセージもしっかり打ち出しています。2018年にはLGBTをターゲットにしたヘイト・スピーチや犯罪が増加し、難民として申請する際にもLGBTだと不許可の割合が多いなど、人権が十分に守られないケースがまだまだ存在します。

　大西洋を挟んだニューヨークでも、6月28日に「ストーンウォールの反乱」から半世紀を記念して、数千人がグリニッジ・ヴィレッジのストーンウォール・インを取り囲みました。各都市のプライド・パレードの主催者も多く参加し、LGBTの人権擁護運動の歴史を、原点に戻って振り返りました。

参考：
https://www.theguardian.com/world/2019/jul/06/london-pride-2019-biggest-yet-say-march-organisers
https://www.nytimes.com/2019/06/28/nyregion/stonewall-inn-50-anniversary.html
https://www.nytimes.com/2019/06/28/nyregion/stonewall-riots-rally.html?action=click&module=pride%20footer%20recirc%20module&pgtype=Article

▶ Watch the news, then fill the gaps in the text.

Newsreader: Britain's biggest ever Pride has been (¹   ) (²   ) in London with an all-singing, all-dancing carnival of colour. Organisers say up to one and a half million people (³   ). This year's event celebrated 50 years since the first Stonewall uprising in New York, where a series of violent (⁴   ) took place between police and gay rights activists. Here's our LGBT correspondent, Ben Hunte. And just a (⁵   ), this report contains some flashing images.

Ben Hunte: (⁶   ), protest and one big party. Pride came to London today, and for many here it was a Saturday like no other.

Hunte: This is believed to be the country's biggest Pride event ever, with (⁷   ) the central theme.

First man: It's an opportunity for us to stand in (⁸   ) and show that, no matter what race, religion, sexuality, we belong, we are Londoners. We have a place here. Everyone is equal.

Second man: Everyone can be whatever they want to be. Whatever they do, is, is up to them. And I think it's really important for a straight, gay, transgender, whatever it is to (⁹   ) (¹⁰   ) and support.

Hunte: More than 30,000 people from across the LGBT community have (¹¹   ) through the streets today. They've come from over 600 organisations and corporations, with many of them marching for the very first time.

Hunte: Organisers estimate that more than 1.5 million people were on the streets of the (¹²   ) to watch the parade today. With homophobic and transphobic attacks on the (¹³   ) across the UK, some activists had called for this year's (¹⁴   ) Pride event to return to its roots as a (¹⁵   ).

Phyllis Aqua Opoku-Gyimah, co-founder, executive director of UK Black Pride:

Whilst we're living in a, a time where there's so much (**16**   ) and (**17**   ) debate over our trans-siblings, we've got to always go back to our history, our her-story and our their-story.

35

Hunte: However, for many of the (**18**   ) we spoke to today, they were just 40 (**19**   ) to have the opportunity to be so (**20**   ) and so proud. Ben Hunte, BBC News.

(Saturday 6 July 2019)

Notes

l.1 **Pride (parade)**「プライド・パレード」レズビアン・ゲイ・バイセクシュアル・トランスジェンダー(LGBT) の文化を讃えるパレード。ストーンウォールの反乱の1周年を記念してアメリカ各地で行われたデモを起源 とする　l.4 **carnival of colour**「色とりどりのカーニバル」プライド・パレードではシンボルとして赤・橙・ 黄・緑・青・紫の6色から成る虹色の旗が掲げられる　l.7 **Stonewall uprising**「ストーンウォールの反乱」 1969年6月28日未明に、アメリカ、ニューヨーク市内グリニッジ・ヴィレッジにあったゲイバー「ストーン ウォール・イン（Stonewall Inn」に警察の弾圧的な手入れが行われたことを契機に起こった数千人規模の 暴動　l.9 **LGBT**(=lesbian, gay, bisexual, transgender) queer（風変わりな）または questioning（自身 の性自認や性的指向が定まっていない）を含めて、近年 LGBTQ と言うことがある　l.27 **estimate**　動詞 なので本来 [éstəmèit] と発音すべきだが、ハントは名詞風に [éstəmət] と発音している　l.28 **homophobic** 「同性愛嫌悪の」　l.28 **transphobic**「トランスジェンダー嫌悪の」　l.34 **UK Black Pride**「UK ブラッ ク・プライド」2005年からロンドンで開催されている黒人 LGBTQ のためのプライド・イベント。ヨーロッ パ最大のアジア、中東、南米、カリブ系の LGBTQ の祭典で、毎年約8,000人が参加する　l.39 **history**「男 性中心の歴史」history を男性所有格 his + story と捉え、これまでの歴史が男性中心であることを指す。そ れに対して、her-story「女性中心の歴史」、their-story「男女両性中心の歴史」という単語が生じた

ありのままに生きる人々

　ゲイ（gay）という言葉は12世紀に古フランス語のgaiから英語として入ってきました。もともとは「陽気な」「気楽な」「気ままな」といった意味で使われていましたが、17世紀頃までには道徳に束縛されないことや享楽に溺れることを表すようになり、次第に性的な意味を帯びるようになっていきます。当初は異性との性的関係を示唆する言葉でしたが、19世紀後半には、同性間、特に男性同士の性的関係を表す俗語として使われるようになりました。その後の1920年代には、同性愛の人々が自らの指向を表すのに用いるようになり、今日のように、自らの生き方を肯定する前向きな用語として定着しました。

Moving On

6 Making a Summary

▶ Fill the gaps to complete the summary.

　The 2019 London Pride parade was the biggest ever, with 1.5 million people attending, and 30,000 marching, many for the first time. It celebrated 50 years since the Stonewall (u　　　　　), and violent (c　　　　　) in New York between the police and gay activists. The central theme of the parade was (d　　　　　). One man said that no matter what race, religion, or sexuality they belong to, they should all stand in (s　　　　　) as Londoners. A woman said everyone is equal, and we should avoid (p　　　　　) and toxic debate. However, (h　　　　　) and (t　　　　　) attacks are increasing in the UK, and some people thought this (f　　　　　) Pride event should return to its roots as a protest.

7 Follow Up

▶ Discuss, write or present.

1. Is there a Pride parade in Japan? Do many people participate? Would you like to participate?

2. The men in the video said that everybody was equal, and everyone can be whatever they want to be. Do you agree with them?

3. The woman at the end of the video said "... we've got to always go back to our history, our her-story, and our their-story". What do you think she meant? Do you think she was joking or was she being serious?

Unit 14

The UN Report on Climate Change

気候変動に対する深刻な報告がなされ、各国政府による早急な対策が必要とされています。
人類には今、何が求められているのでしょうか？ニュースを見てみましょう。

Starting Off

1 Setting the Scene

▶ **What do you think?**

1. What do we mean by 'climate change'? How is it caused? Are you worried about it?

2. What are governments doing to stop climate change, or protect us from climate change? Do you think they are doing enough?

3. What can you personally do to help solve the problem? Do you think you are doing enough?

2 Building Language

▶ **Which word (1-8) best fits which explanation (a-h)?**

1. curb   [   ]   a. can't be maintained without causing ecological damage
2. unsustainable   [   ]   b. feed on grass, like cattle or sheep
3. wreck   [   ]   c. throw away, reject, get rid of
4. sweeping   [   ]   d. comprehensive and wide-ranging
5. graze   [   ]   e. reduce or limit
6. fraught   [   ]   f. completely destroy
7. degrade   [   ]   g. tense, full of stress, worrying
8. discard   [   ]   h. reduce in strength or quality

Watching the News

3 Understanding Check 1

▶ Read the quotes, then watch the news and match them to the right people.

1. ... then we could have significant benefits for the climate, but also for our health. [ ]

2. And that message may not go down very well here ... [ ]

3. ... humanity faces increasingly painful trade-offs between food security, and rising temperatures ... [ ]

4. ... an increasingly desperate attempt to stop the planet overheating. [ ]

4 Understanding Check 2

▶ Which is the best answer?

1. What effects do cattle have on our environment?
   a. Cattle have more environmental benefits than growing plant protein.
   b. Cattle allow us to produce food from poor soil, but their burps create greenhouse gases.
   c. Cattle suck carbon dioxide from the atmosphere and regulate the climate.
   d. Cattle require low-intensity grazing, which does not heat the atmosphere as much as forests.

2. What are the scientists in the Alps saying about our diet?
   a. We must eat less red meat and dairy produce, and more vegetables.
   b. In order to stop global warming, everybody must become vegan.
   c. Regions which are heavily dependent on cheese and meat need not go vegan.
   d. Veganism is not good for you, because we need to eat meat.

3. Which of the following recommendations was not mentioned in the video?
   a. We should feed people in ways that don't cause desertification by over-grazing.
   b. We should not grow so many trees to make electricity.
   c. We should stop destroying our forests.
   d. We should grow more of our own food in our gardens.

▶ **What do you remember?**

4. According to the recent major report on climate what must we do?

_____

5. How is the Geneva charity redistributing waste food?

_____

6. What is happening to the peat moors in the north of England?

_____

BACKGROUND INFORMATION

　2019年8月2日から7日にかけて、「気候変動に関する政府間パネル（IPCC: Intergovernmental Panel on Climate Change)」の第50回会合（IPCC-50）が、スイスのジュネーヴで開催されました。IPCCは、国際連合（UN: United Nations）と世界気象機関（WMO: World Meteorological Organization）によって1988年に設立された組織です。気候変動や地球温暖化の影響とその緩和対策などについて科学的見地から評価を行うことを目的としており、現在195国が加盟しています。

　今回の会合には、120を超える国々から350名以上が参加し、気候変動に関する最新の報告である「気候変動と土地に関する特別報告書（the Special Report on Climate Change and Land)」の検討と承認を行いました。この報告は、人間の土地の利用方法がどのように気候変動の要因になっているか、そして、気候変動が土地にどのような影響を与えているかをまとめたもので、資源としての土地の持続的な管理、砂漠化や土地の劣化の問題、食糧安全保障、陸上の生態系における温室効果ガスの変動などについて述べています。土地は人間の生活に必要不可欠であり、水や食料など生態系に由来するたくさんの恩恵を私たちに与えてくれます。人類による土地の利用は現在、氷のない陸の地表の約70％以上に影響を与えており、人口増加と1人あたりの食料、飼料、繊維、木材、エネルギーの消費量の増大によって、土地や水の利用が急速に進んでいると言われています。気候変動によって土地や生態系に変化が起きることで、急激に増加する人口を養うための資源の確保が難しくなり、世界的な危機が訪れることが懸念されているのです。

　気候変動に歯止めをかけるべく様々な方法が模索されていますが、一方で、2020年のコロナウイルスの流行により、世界の一部の地域で、温室効果ガスや大気中の汚染物質の量が一時的に激減したという研究もあります。人間の経済活動や移動が制限されたことによる効果とみられ、例えば、中国では大気汚染物質の排出量やエネルギーの使用量が2週間で25％減少しました。また、ニューヨークでも、交通量の減少により、空気中の一酸化炭素が50％減少したことが報告されています。人間の生産活動を維持しつつ、地球環境を守っていくにはどうすればよいのか、先の見えない議論が続いています。

参考：
https://enb.iisd.org/vol12/enb12760e.html
https://www.ipcc.ch/srccl/chapter/summary-for-policymakers/
https://www.bbc.com/news/science-environment-51944780

▶ **Watch the news, then fill the gaps in the text.**

Newsreader: A major report on climate change warns humanity faces increasingly painful trade-offs between food security, and rising temperatures, within decades, unless it (^{1}) emissions and stops (^{2}) farming and

5

deforestation. The UN's Intergovernmental Panel on Climate Change has warned that efforts to limit global warming, while feeding a booming population, could be (^{3}) without swift and (^{4}) changes to how we use the land we live off. Here's our environment correspondent, Roger Harrabin.   10

Roger Harrabin: This Alpine landscape was once covered by forest. The trees (^{5}) carbon dioxide from the atmosphere and regulated the climate. Then humans cleared some of the land for food. But cattle burp methane and that strongly heats the atmosphere. This sort of low-intensity (^{6}) may produce protein from poor soil, and it does have some environmental (^{7}), but it still creates more greenhouse gasses than growing plant protein.

15

Harrabin: Scientists meeting here in the Alps are not saying we've all got to go vegan to protect the climate. They are saying that we do need to cut down on red meat and dairy (^{8}) and shift on towards eating more vegetables. And that message may not go down very well here in a region that is so heavily dependent on cheese and meat.   20   25

Harrabin: Debate here has been (^{9}) because the way we use the land is so complex. Among the experts' recommendations are, on biofuels: limiting the area used to grow trees to be burned to make electricity. This could (^{10}) with feeding the world. On deforestation: working harder to protect the trees that protect us from climate heating. On desertification: finding ways to feed people, that don't involve (^{11}) the soil through (^{12}).
Then there's the way we eat.

30

35

Professor Pete Smith, Chair in Plant & Soil Science, University of Aberdeen: In the West, we can, we overconsume meat and dairy. Er, that's bad for our health. It's bad for the climate. It's bad for water. It's bad for land (^{13}). So if we were able to reduce our (^{14}), um, in the West, of meat and dairy, then we could have significant benefits for the climate, but also for our health.

40

Harrabin: Scientists also want to stop food being (^{15}), because wasting food means the greenhouse gasses, created to produce the fertilizers to grow the crops, have been for nothing. A charity in Geneva redistributes waste food. Here they're taking stale bread, and turning it into new cookies. This avoids having to produce fresh (^{16}) to make the cookies.

45

Harrabin: Here's a positive sign. These peat moors in the north of England were previously drained so animals can (^{17}). When peat's (^{18}) to the air, it gives off greenhouse gasses. So now they're blocking up the channels to (^{19}) the peat again. One of the easier options in what, for scientists, has become an increasingly desperate attempt to stop the planet overheating. Roger Harrabin, BBC News.

50

55

(Thursday 8 August 2019)

Notes

l.7 **Intergovernmental Panel on Climate Change**「気候変動に関する政府間パネル（IPCC）」人為起源による気候変化、影響、適応及び緩和方策に関し、科学的、技術的、社会経済学的な見地から包括的な評価を行うことを目的として、1988 年に世界気象機関（WMO）と国連環境計画（UNEP）により設立された組織　l.20 **Scientists meeting here in the Alps**「ここアルプスで会合を開いている科学者たち」スイスのジュネーヴで開かれている会合のこと〈p. 81 参照〉　l.36 **Plant & Soil Science**「植物土壌科学」遺伝子組み換えやバイオテクノロジーを含む植物や土壌を研究する科学　l.37 **University of Aberdeen**「アバディーン大学」スコットランドのアバディーンにある大学。1495 年に設立された大学を前身とする

様々なヴィーガンたち

　地球環境に優しいとされる「ヴィーガン（Vegan）」は、「菜食主義者（Vegetarian）」よりも制約の厳しい食生活を送り、肉、魚、卵、乳製品、蜂蜜といった動物性の食品を一切口にしない完全菜食主義者です。1944年にイギリスで発祥しましたが、近年の世界的な流行により、その様式はますます細分化されてきています。「倫理的ヴィーガン（Ethical Vegan）」は衣食住全てにおいて動物性のものを避ける人たち、「食生活ヴィーガン（Dietary Vegan）」は植物性のものだけを食べますが、衣類などに含まれる動物性のものは良しとする人たち、「東洋的ヴィーガン（Oriental Vegan）」はネギ属以外の植物性食品を食する人たち、「非加熱ヴィーガン（Raw Vegan）」は酵素が壊れないよう低温調理した植物性食品のみを食する人たち、そして「環境的ヴィーガン（Environmental Vegan）」は産業が環境に悪影響を及ぼしているという理由で動物性のものを排除する人たちです。

Moving On

6 Making a Summary

CD2-19

▶ Fill the gaps to complete the summary.

　　The United Nations Intergovernmental Panel on Climate Change has warned that we must (c　　　　　) emissions and stop (u　　　　　　　　　) farming and deforestation. Unless we make (s　　　　　) changes to how we use our land, our efforts to limit global warming could be (w　　　　　). One important change is in what we grow to eat. Cattle that are (g　　　　　　) produce methane, which is a greenhouse gas, so we should cut down on red meat and dairy foods. We should instead find ways to feed ourselves that don't involve (d　　　　　) the soil through over-(g　　　　　). Vegetables are much better both for us and for the climate. However, the debate is (f　　　　　) because some regions are very dependent on cheese and meat. Scientists also want to stop food being (d　　　　　), and one charity turns stale bread into new cookies. One positive sign is that peat moors in England are being soaked so that they no longer give off greenhouse gasses.

7 Follow Up

▶ Discuss, write or present.

1. How much red meat or dairy produce do you eat? Do you think you could eat less in order to stop global warming?

2. Do you waste much food? What about shops and restaurants in Japan? What could they do with food they don't need, instead of throwing it away?

3. The report said we must make painful decisions "within decades." Are you optimistic that we will be able to limit global warming? Explain your opinion.

Unit 15

Facial Recognition in London Streets

ロンドン警視庁が最新式のカメラを使用することを検討しています。どのように利用し、どのような問題があるのでしょうか。ニュースを見てみましょう。

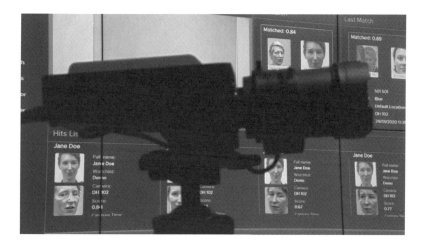

Starting Off

1 Setting the Scene

▶ What do you think?

1. Do you feel safe when you are walking around the streets of your town?
2. Do you think the police are doing a good job in keeping the public safe? Is there anything that you think they should do?
3. What technology do the police use in order to keep you safe?

2 Building Language

▶ For each word (1-7), find two synonyms (a-n).

1. oversee   [   ] [   ]
2. entitlement [   ] [   ]
3. unveil   [   ] [   ]
4. discreet   [   ] [   ]
5. instantaneous [   ] [   ]
6. discernible [   ] [   ]
7. authoritarian [   ] [   ]

a. right
b. supervise
c. disclose
d. reveal
e. strict
f. recognisable
g. permit
h. distinct
i. inspect
j. dictatorial
k. cautious
l. rapid
m. prudent
n. immediate

3 Understanding Check 1

▶ **Read the quotes, then watch the news and match them to the right people.**

1. We don't have that kind of culture here.   [   ]

2. ... live facial recognition cameras could be coming to a street near you.   [   ]

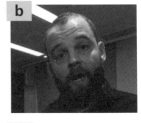

3. There'll be two cameras, like this, based on wherever the operation is taking place.   [   ]

4. ... you'll clearly be aware that your image is being captured ...   [   ]

4 Understanding Check 2

▶ **Which is the best answer?**

1. What is this video mainly about?
    a. Thanks to new cameras, serious crime in London has decreased.
    b. Despite much opposition, the police will install facial recognition cameras.
    c. People are being encouraged to be more discreet when they photograph faces.
    d. Because of opposition, the police won't install facial recognition cameras.

2. What happened with the trial at Notting Hill?
    a. It failed because it was too crowded.
    b. It was instantaneously deleted.
    c. It lasted for two years, and found that crowds were dense.
    d. Some serious and violent criminals were missing.

3. Which of the following sentences is correct, according to the video?
    a. The police claim that the cameras can falsely identify people from different ethnic groups.
    b. An independent group found that the cameras only spotted 70% of suspects, but the police disagreed.
    c. The police found that 70% of suspects came from different ethnic groups.
    d. The police say that the cameras are successful 70% of the time, but a review concluded they were less accurate.

86

4. What concerns have been raised about the use of facial recognition cameras?

_____

5. What should happen if your picture is taken by the Met's facial recognition cameras but you are not a criminal or missing person?

_____

6. According to the woman at the end of the video, why can't the police demand that we show our identity cards?

_____

BACKGROUND INFORMATION

　近年では、家庭用のデジタルカメラやSNSの顔認識機能さえもが高度な性能を備えるようになりました。ロンドン警視庁は、そのような技術を捜査に利用し、治安維持に役立てると発表しました。ロンドン警視庁と南ウェールズ警察が合同で導入を進めてきたカメラは、日本の大手電子通信機器メーカー NEC が開発した生物測定学に基づいた顔認識システムで、二次元の写真を人工知能で解析して三次元の像を導き出し、個人を特定する機能を備えています。

　イギリスはCCTV（closed-circuit television）カメラの設置台数が世界一で、その歴史も長く、最初に警備目的で監視カメラが使われたのは、1960年のタイ国王の訪問にまで遡ります。その後、アメリカの警備会社がカメラ設置を普及させ、各国で一般的になりました。また、2001年に開始したグーグルアースでは、ネット上で世界を巡れるようになりました。

　しかし、警察が顔認識システムを導入することに対して、プライバシーや人権が侵害されることを危惧する人もいます。2015年6月以降、ロンドン、南ウェールズ、レスター州の警察が、顔認識システムを試験的に導入してきました。イベントの警備に顔認識カメラが使われ、多くの人が集まるスタジアムでのスポーツの試合やデモ行進などにカメラが向けられました。南ウェールズでは、カメラに2度捉えられた地方自治体のエド・ブリッジズ(Ed Bridges)議員が警察に対して訴訟を起こしましたが、カーディフの高等法院は警察による顔認識技術の使用を合法としました。警察は限定的な使用を強調していますが、法の整備を求める声が多く聞かれます。

　2020年は新型コロナウイルスが世界中で猛威を振るい、経済活動が停滞を余儀無くされましたが、第2波に備えAIによる検温を取り入れる企業が増加しています。捜索のために開発された顔認証技術は、新たな活路を開いています。

参考：
https://www.theguardian.com/technology/2020/jan/24/what-is-facial-recognition-and-how-do-police-use-it
https://www.bbc.com/news/uk-48315979
https://stories.swns.com/news/history-cctv-surveillance-britain-93449/
https://www.bbc.com/news/uk-wales-49565287

5 Filling Gaps | News Story |

▶ **Watch the news, then fill the gaps in the text.**

Newsreader: So, for the first time, live facial recognition cameras could be coming to a street near you. But will they help keep us safe from crime, or are they a (¹   ) to our privacy? The Met says it will use them for specific targets. People want it for serious and violent crimes, but some

5

have raised concerns about how accurate they are and whether (²   ) people could be picked out by mistake. And there are now calls for new laws to be introduced to (³   ) this technology. James Waterhouse has this report.   10

James Waterhouse: It's a tricky, legal balance. The rights of the police to do their job, versus someone's (⁴   ) to a private life. It's rarely been tested more than with facial recognition cameras.

Waterhouse: Today, the Metropolitan Police excitedly (⁵   ) the model which will be appearing on London's streets for the first time.   15

Waterhouse: So here's how it works. There'll be two cameras, like this, based on wherever the operation is taking place. If someone walks through and they're not on the watch list they'll appear (⁶   ), and subsequently be deleted from the system. If there's a match, there'll be a (⁷   ). And officers can then decide whether to approach that person.   20

Nick Ephgrave, Assistant Commissioner, Metropolitan Police: The cameras are located, um, fairly (⁸   ), so it's not about having a camera in your face, but you'll clearly be aware that your image is being captured, processed, and if you're not, er, matched to one of the watch list images that we have on the that database on that day, then it's (⁹   ) deleted.   25

Waterhouse: The force has been trying it out for two years. At Notting Hill it found the crowds were too (¹⁰   ), but it's keen to stress it'll only be targeting specific areas based on evidence. Their targets: serious or violent criminals, and (¹¹   ) people.

Waterhouse: The history of police forces using this technology isn't great. Most recently there were claims black people and those from an ethnic minority could be (¹²   ) identified because police didn't test how it worked on faces that weren't white.

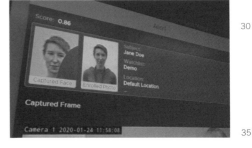

30

35

88

Ephgrave: The ten trials we've done have shown no (^{13}) difference in this algorithm's ability to identify people from different ethnic groups.

Waterhouse: The Met claims it has a 70% hit rate for (^{14}) suspects, although an independent review found a much lower (^{15}). Campaign groups like Liberty and Big Brother have (^{16}) legal action, calling it a serious attack on individual freedoms.

Woman: The police have considerable powers to (^{17}) with your freedom and they're only supposed to do so when there's an (^{18}) reason. And that's why we have things like (^{19}). That's why they can't just go around and demand that you show your papers and your identity cards. We don't have that kind of culture here. That's what you would expect in an (^{20}) country.

Waterhouse: The Met's previously been (^{21}) to talk about this technology, but things are different now. A (^{22}) of government support, along with police in South Wales recently seeing off a High Court challenge, means it feels able to make the leap. James Waterhouse, BBC London.

(Friday 24 January 2020)

Notes

l.5 **The Met**「ロンドン警視庁」イギリスの警察組織の1つ。首都ロンドン一円を管轄する首都警察であると同時に、国家全体の警備や王族、政府の要人の警護を行う。通称スコットランドヤードと呼ばれる
l.26 **Notting Hill**「ノッティングヒル」ロンドン西部に位置する閑静な住宅街。カーニバルやアンティーク・マーケットで有名　l.38 **algorithm**「アルゴリズム」ある特定の問題を解いたり、課題を解決したりするための計算手順や処理手順を定式化した形で表現したもの　l.43 **Liberty**「リバティ」不正に立ち向かい、自由を守り、全てのイギリス国民が公平に扱われることを目指す人権擁護団体。1934年設立　l.43 **Big Brother** (=Big Brother Watch)「ビッグ・ブラザー・ウォッチ」自由を不当に侵害する監視国家に反対し、イギリス国民の自由を守ろうとするNPO団体。2009年設立　l.53 **along with police in South Wales recently seeing off a High Court challenge**「南ウェールズの警察が最近、高等法院での異議申し立てをかわしたことと一緒になって」2019年5月にエド・ブリッジズが起こした顔認識カメラを巡る裁判を指す〈p.87参照〉

犯人の顔写真、マグショット

　犯罪の容疑者を逮捕後に撮影した写真のことを「マグショット（mugshot）」と呼びます。英語でmugとは「顔」を表す俗語です。簡素な壁や身長を表す目盛りを背景に、正面と側面から犯人を写した顔写真は、ニュースや犯罪ドキュメンタリー、テレビドラマなどでよく見かけます。最古のマグショットは、1840年代にベルギーで撮影された囚人の写真であると言われており、イギリスでもバーミンガムの警察が1850年代に導入を開始しました。1880年代には、フランスの警察官僚だったアルフォンス・ベルティヨン（Alphonse Bertillon, 1853-1914）によって撮影の手法が標準化され、各国で取り入れられるようになりました。

Moving On

6 Making a Summary

CD2-22

▶ **Fill the gaps to complete the summary.**

　　There are soon going to be more facial recognition cameras on London streets, and the police have just (u　　　　　) the camera that will be used. They say that they are only targeting serious or violent criminals, or missing people. However, some people say we need new laws to (o　　　　　) this technology, and we must respect a person's (e　　　　　) to a private life. One concern is that they might not be accurate and ethnic minorities might be falsely identified. However, the police say it is 70% accurate and there is no (d　　　　　) difference in identifications from different ethnic groups. One woman pointed out that Britain was not an (a　　　　　) country, so the police can only (i　　　　　) with our freedom if they have warrant cards. However, the police claim that the cameras will be (d　　　　　) and if a person is not on the police database, their photo will be (i　　　　　) deleted.

7 Follow Up

▶ **Discuss, write or present.**

1. How do you feel about facial recognition cameras? Do you think they are necessary to protect us from crime, or are they a threat to our privacy and freedom?

2. The police want to use the cameras to catch criminals and find missing people. But there are other uses for these cameras. Can you think of some?

3. At the end, the woman said that Britain was not an authoritarian country. Do you know of any countries that are authoritarian? Would you like to live in such countries? How would life be different?

このテキストのメインページ
www.kinsei-do.co.jp/plusmedia/411

次のページの QR コードを読み取る
直接ページにジャンプできます

オンライン映像配信サービス「plus+Media」について

本テキストの映像は plus+Media ページ（www.kinsei-do.co.jp/plusmedia）から、ストリーミング再生でご利用いただけます。手順は以下に従ってください。

ログイン

● ご利用には、ログインが必要です。
　サイトのログインページ（www.kinsei-do.co.jp/plusmedia/login）へ行き、plus+Media パスワード（次のページのシールをはがしたあとに印字されている数字とアルファベット）を入力します。

● パスワードは各テキストにつき1つです。
　有効期限は、はじめてログインした時点から1年間になります。

ログインページ

[利用方法]

次のページにある QR コード、もしくは plus+Media トップページ（www.kinsei-do.co.jp/plusmedia）から該当するテキストを選んで、そのテキストのメインページにジャンプしてください。

メニューページ
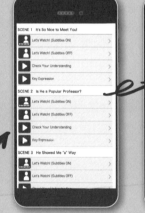

再生画面

plus+Media トップ　　　　メインページ

「Video」「Audio」をタッチすると、それぞれのメニューページにジャンプしますので、そこから該当する項目を選べば、ストリーミングが開始されます。

[推奨環境]

iOS (iPhone, iPad)	OS: iOS 6 〜 13 ブラウザ：標準ブラウザ	Android	OS: Android 4.x 〜 10.0 ブラウザ：標準ブラウザ、Chrome
PC	OS: Windows 7/8/8.1/10, MacOS X　**ブラウザ:** Internet Explorer 10/11, Microsoft Edge, Firefox 48以降, Chrome 53以降, Safari		

※最新の推奨環境についてはウェブサイトをご確認ください。
※上記の推奨環境を満たしている場合でも、機種によってはご利用いただけない場合もあります。また、推奨環境は技術動向等により変更される場合があります。予めご了承ください。

このシールをはがすと
plus+Media 利用のための
パスワードが
記載されています。

一度はがすと元に戻すことは
できませんのでご注意下さい。

◀ここからはがして下さい

4116 British News
Update 3
(BBC)

plus+Media

本書にはCD（別売）があります

British News Update 3

映像で学ぶ　イギリス公共放送の最新ニュース3

2021年1月20日　初版第1刷発行
2021年2月20日　初版第2刷発行

編著者　Timothy Knowles

田　村　真　弓

田　中　みんね

中　村　美帆子

発行者　　福　岡　正　人

発行所　　株式会社　金　星　堂

（〒101-0051）東京都千代田区神田神保町 3-21
Tel　（03）3263-3828（営業部）
　　　（03）3263-3997（編集部）
Fax　（03）3263-0716
http://www.kinsei-do.co.jp

編集担当　長島吉成　　　　　　　　　Printed in Japan
印刷所・製本所／三美印刷株式会社

ISBN978-4-7647-4116-4　C1082